COOKING ON THE
INDOOR GRILL

Catherine Pagano Fulde

BRISTOL PUBLISHING ENTERPRISES
San Leandro, California

A **nitty gritty**® Cookbook

Printed in the United States of America.

ISBN: 1-55867-266-4

Cover design: Frank J. Paredes
Cover photography: John A. Benson
Food stylist: Susan Devaty
Illustrator: Grant Corley

CONTENTS

INDOOR GRILLING WITH THE ELECTRIC CONTACT GRILL

Grilling indoors is not a new concept. People who enjoy the taste of freshly grilled foods want the option to grill year round, whatever the weather. The flat electric indoor grill, introduced in the 1960s, was the first attempt to approximate the grilling method so popular outdoors. Grilling stones and skillet grills (frying pans with parallel raised ridges on the bottom designed to simulate grill marks) followed. Unfortunately, there were some inconveniences about using such grills. Not all were smokeless or easy to clean. But now the indoor grill combines both smokeless cooking and easy cleanup.

The indoor electric contact grill is hinged like a clam shell with ridged grids on top and below. Its design is similar to that of a waffle iron. When preheated for 5 to 15 minutes, the contact grill cooks food in a fraction of the time it takes on a standard flat grill. Imagine cooking most meats, fish and poultry in less than 5 minutes! They emerge from the grill delicately crusted, brown and juicy. Most vegetables cook crisp-tender with pale grill marks and a slight glaze. Fruit becomes special when grilled, since the natural sugars caramelize and intensify its sweetness. Because of the short cooking time, there are no "flare-ups" and no smoke.

Contact grill grids generally have a nonstick surface and clean up easily with a damp paper towel. Some foods in sweet marinades tend to leave a sticky residue on the grids, but a little mild soap on a soft brush, followed by a wet paper towel, takes care of the cleanup. The removable drip pans, grids and spatulas are usually dishwasher-safe—check your owner's manual to make sure.

HELPFUL HINTS FOR FOOD PREPARATION

Since foods cook so quickly on the indoor grill, it is important that side dishes, sauces and other food preparation be done first. Most cooked foods can be held in a 250° oven while grilling main dishes. Because the grilling time is so short, there is no fear that these foods will dry out. It is a good idea to also heat serving plates while the oven is at this gentle setting.

Preparation is important when grilling. Preheating the indoor grill is necessary to create faster browning. Always mist a cold grill with nonfat cooking spray or vegetable oil spray. Brushing oil on the cold grids with a pastry brush or paper towel also helps to keep the nonstick surface slick. Bring refrigerated food to room temperature before grilling. While the grill is heating, place foods to be cooked, their seasoning and garnishes on paper towels or in small bowls near the grill. Have a serving platter ready to hold the cooked food so it can be removed from the grill at the precise time it is ready. Sometimes a minute extra on the hot grill makes the difference between succulent and dry food.

Cooking at such high temperatures requires care. Use pot holders when opening the grill. Hot air and steam accumulates inside the covered grill, so open slowly and carefully to prevent burns.

Foods best suited for the contact grill are meats, poultry and fish that are boneless and cut under 2 inches thick. Raw vegetables cook best when cut $1/4$-inch to $1/2$-inch thick. With densely textured or fleshy vegetables, it is best to blanch or parboil before grilling. This is especially true when using vegetables in kabobs. Because of the intense heat, dense food will char on the outside before cooking tender on the inside.

MEATS

"Sizzling Sirloin Steak!" The sound and aroma of a beef steak cooking to perfection says it all about the contact grill. Tender steak is by far the most popular food prepared in the grill. This method of fast cooking sears the outside while allowing the interior to remain pink and juicy. Whether it is rare, medium or well done, steak is prized for its robust flavor and hefty "mouth feel." Loin cuts like filet mignon, New York strip steak, T-bone and porterhouse steaks are the most desirable. Top sirloin, London broil, tri-tip and skirt steak benefit from a marinade which, in addition to adding flavor, helps soften the meat, making it more tender.

Pork, lamb and veal, like beef, are most delicious when prepared in the grill. Select the more tender cuts of these meats for grilling, but remember, boneless meat cooks best in the contact grill. Slices of pork tenderloin and boneless lamb leg are good choices.

Keep in mind the following hints for grilling success. Wipe meat with a damp paper towel, remove as much fat as possible and bring to room temperature before grilling. Do not use cuts of meat thicker than 2 inches for even cooking. Ribs, chops and any other meat with a small bone will grill if thinly cut. Preheat the grill for 10 to 15 minutes before cooking meat. Always wash the platter containing the raw meat before placing cooked meat on it. If you use a marinade as a sauce for cooked meats, be sure to boil and strain it before serving.

Determine the doneness of meats using an instant-read thermometer or by touch (using a fork to press the meat). Rare meat (140°) is soft to the touch; medium meat (160°) springs back when touched; well done meat (170°) is firm to the touch. Rest large steaks away from the heat for a few minutes after cooking so the juices return to the interior of the steak.

FISH AND SEAFOOD

Fish and seafood are naturals for cooking in the contact grill since they cook quickly and flavorfully with hardly any preparation. Select fresh or frozen fish with the idea of cooking it within 24 hours. Defrost frozen fish in the refrigerator to help keep its texture firm. Wash fish under cold running water and dry with paper towels. Always mist the cold grill with cooking spray or oil and preheat before cooking. The oil prevents the tender-skinned fish from sticking to the grill. If fish or seafood is of a delicate texture, coat well with oil, season and then grill. A general rule for cooking fish in the contact grill is to allow 5 minutes per inch of thickness, remembering to choose fillets that are well less than 2 inches thick. Look for opaque flesh in the thickest part of the fish to determine doneness.

POULTRY

With the emphasis on healthful eating, chicken has become a universal favorite. This is especially true with grilling, since chicken is vying with red meat in popularity. Boneless, skinless chicken breasts are receptive to aromatic marinades and rubs. When quickly grilled, they remain juicy and succulent, retaining the layered flavors of the herbs and spices used in the marinade. Lovers of dark meat will enjoy the quick cooking that seals in the robust flavors. Remember to keep the flesh flat so the chicken will cook evenly.

Turkey breast slices, duck breast halves, Cornish hens and other small birds will cook evenly, despite the bones, if they are flattened. This is easily accomplished for small birds by tucking the wings behind the breast, placing the halves between sheets of plastic wrap and gently pounding with a meat mallet.

Wash poultry under running water and dry thoroughly before proceeding with preparations. Keep thickness less than 1½ inches for super-fast grilling. Most poultry cooks in less than 4 minutes on the contact grill. Its flesh will be golden brown and firm to the touch when cooked.

VEGETABLES

There is nothing to equal the rich flavor of grilled vegetables. Brushed with olive oil, sprinkled with salt and pepper and quickly cooked in the contact grill, they are simply delicious. When marinated with spices, herbs, citrus, oils, vinegars and other condiments, they become food for the gods!

Most vegetables can be grilled. Some benefit from blanching or parboiling first. Hard, dense vegetables like potatoes and carrots or fleshy ones like bell peppers and artichokes should be quickly blanched to the crisp-tender stage. Leafy vegetables like cabbage and radicchio are novelties to the American grill, although they are standard fare in some European countries.

Cooking vegetables in the contact grill takes somewhat longer than meats, fish and poultry. For success with vegetables, be sure to keep slices even in thickness—¼- to ½-inch seems to work best. Cook on a well-lubricated grill and watch carefully.

FRUIT

Any fruit that tastes good heated will do fine on the grill. After all, heat solidifies the sugars and produces an intense flavor. With the exception of citrus, most fruit tastes more rich and concentrated when warmed in the contact grill.

MARINADES AND RUBS

Basic food takes on a variety of complex flavors when enhanced by marinades and rubs. The combinations of spices, herbs, oils, wines, vinegars and syrups are endless; therefore the resulting tastes of marinated food are endless. The intense heat of the contact grill bonds the marinade ingredients and seals these flavors in the basic food, producing great taste sensations.

Many of the recipes which follow present foods marinated or rubbed with spice and herb combinations that are based on popular tastes. As more Americans travel overseas and bring back a taste for foreign flavors, food markets carry a greater variety of commercially prepared marinades and rubs using exotic spice blends. Many of them are excellent and are lifesavers when time is short.

ABOUT THE RECIPES

One of the attractions of cooking with an indoor contact grill is the speed with which food is cooked. The recipes which follow are quick to assemble and fast to prepare. Some recipes require in-and-out time; that is, in the kitchen to mix the marinade (or purchase a similar one) and refrigerate; out for free time; then back again to grill it. Others require you to mix and marinade overnight; and still others require you to season and grill the food. With all the time we are saving in the kitchen, remember what a famous chef once remarked: "The best seasoning is love; a happy cook is a good cook." Have fun with these recipes!

APPETIZERS

10	Grilled Won Ton Wrappers
11	Won Ton Pizza
12	Bruschetta
13	Summer Tomato With Dried Oregano
14	Roasted Garlic With Tuscan-Style Beans
15	Radicchio With Gorgonzola Cheese and Hazelnuts
16	Cantaloupe With Prosciutto
17	Grilled Halloumi Cheese
18	Halloumi Cheese With Cherry Tomatoes
19	Spicy Eggplant Rounds
20	Stuffed Thai Leeks With Ginger Dipping Sauce
22	Coconut Shrimp
23	Baby Octopus Oregano
24	Spicy Cocktail Kabobs
25	Tofu With Rosemary
26	Bourbon Tofu Fingers
27	Herbed Rice Cakes

GRILLED WON TON WRAPPERS

Won ton wrappers become puffy and crisp when grilled. They make an unusual nibble either plain or seasoned with ethnic spices.

olive oil spray
18 won ton wrappers
commercially prepared seasoning mix, such as Mexican, Italian, Japanese, etc.

Mist the cold grill with olive oil and heat for 10 minutes. Separate won ton wrappers and sprinkle with seasoning. Grill in batches for 4 minutes or until crisp and puffy with light grill marks.

WON TON PIZZA

Another quick appetizer made with won ton wrappers is this zesty double-crusted pizza.

olive oil spray
1/4 cup commercially prepared tomato and basil sauce
2 tbs. anchovy paste
1/4 cup shredded mozzarella cheese
Italian seasoning to taste
30 round won ton wrappers
1 cup water

Mist the cold grill with olive oil and heat for 10 minutes. In a bowl, mix tomato sauce, anchovy paste, cheese and seasoning. On a work surface, separate won ton wrappers. Spread 1 spoonful of the tomato sauce mixture on 1 won ton wrapper. Moisten edges with water. Top with second won ton wrapper and press down around edge to seal. Continue until all won ton wrappers are used. Grill for 6 minutes.

BRUSCHETTA

French or Italian bread toasted in the grill, rubbed with a torn garlic clove and anointed with olive oil, forms the base for a variety of toppings. Let your creativity reign supreme.

1 slim loaf French or Italian bread, cut into ¾-inch-thick slices
4 cloves garlic, peeled and torn in half
3 tbs. extra virgin olive oil

Arrange bread slices on the heated grill and toast in batches for 3 to 4 minutes each. Check for doneness after 2 minutes. Bread will be light gold in color with grill marks. It will be crunchy on the outside but soft on the inside. While still warm, rub each slice with garlic and brush with oil. Use as a base for the toppings that follow on pages 13 and 14.

SUMMER TOMATO WITH DRIED OREGANO

This recipe makes a good bruschetta topping, and a great simple summer salad.

3 vine-ripened summer tomatoes
2 tbs. extra virgin olive oil
1 tsp. dried oregano
sea salt and freshly ground black pepper

Cut tomatoes into a fine dice. In a small serving bowl, mix tomatoes, oil, oregano, salt and pepper. Let stand for at least 30 minutes before using.

ROASTED GARLIC
WITH TUSCAN-STYLE BEANS

Tuscany is one of the most beautiful regions in Italy, and has produced many famous wines and olive oils. This is a typical Tuscan side dish to serve with grilled food or as a bruschetta topping. Chianti is optional.

2 bulbs garlic, top ½ inch removed
5 tbs. extra virgin olive oil
2 cans (15 oz. each) small white beans, rinsed and drained
1 tbs. minced fresh rosemary leaves
salt and freshly ground pepper to taste

Heat oven to 400.° Place garlic bulbs on foil, drizzle 1 tbs. of the oil over each, bring foil up to cover bulbs and bake until tender, about 45 minutes. Remove from oven and cool. When ready, squeeze garlic from skins into a blender container. Add remaining 3 tbs. oil, beans, rosemary, salt and pepper. Whirl mixture to blend, but do not puree; mixture should have texture. Turn into a serving dish. Let stand for 30 minutes for flavors to blend.

RADICCHIO WITH GORGONZOLA AND HAZELNUTS

Serve with bruschetta or arrange whole slices topped with cheese mixture and olive oil as an appetizer.

1/3 cup crumbled soft Gorgonzola cheese
2 tbs. balsamic vinegar
1/3 cup ground toasted hazelnuts
2 small heads radicchio, about 12 oz.
2 tbs. extra virgin olive oil
salt and freshly ground pepper to taste

Heat the grill for 15 minutes. In a small serving bowl, mix cheese, vinegar and hazelnuts. Mixture will be crumbly. Set aside. Cut radicchio lengthwise into 1-inch-thick slices. In a shallow dish, mix oil, salt and pepper. Dip radicchio slices into oil mixture to coat. Grill for 3 minutes, until tender. Remove core, dice and mix with cheese mixture. Drizzle with remaining oil.

CANTALOUPE WITH PROSCIUTTO

Grilled cantaloupe brings a new taste to this favorite international appetizer. The natural sweetness of the melon is intensified by the grilling and provides a hot, sweet contrast to the cool, salty prosciutto. Take care not to overcook.

1 medium cantaloupe
2 oz. prosciutto

Cut cantaloupe in half. Remove seeds, but not rind. Cut each half into 1-inch-thick crescent-shaped slices. Warm on the grill for 1 minute. Remove rind, drape with prosciutto and serve warm.

GRILLED HALLOUMI CHEESE

Halloumi is a salty, firm cheese from Cyprus that grills crusty on the outside and soft on the inside. It is sold in Middle Eastern markets. Served with raw honey and fresh mint, it makes an unusual appetizer. Kalamata olives, melon and fresh figs are good accompaniments. Provolone cheese can be substituted for Halloumi. Grill the provolone for only 1 minute.

3 pita breads
$\frac{1}{2}$ cup raw honey
$\frac{1}{4}$ lb. Halloumi cheese
olive oil for brushing
12–15 fresh mint leaves

Cut each pita bread into 4 pieces. On a hot grill, toast bread for 2 minutes. Set aside and keep warm. Pour honey into a small cup on a serving platter. Remove cheese from wrapper and rinse under cold water for several minutes to remove extra salt. Dry and cut into twelve $\frac{1}{2}$-inch-thick slices. Brush with oil and grill for 3 minutes, until golden brown. Place around honey cup on serving plate. Garnish with mint leaves. To eat: open pita, insert slice of grilled Halloumi and top with a drizzle of honey and a mint leaf.

HALLOUMI CHEESE
WITH CHERRY TOMATOES

Skewers of Halloumi cheese and cherry tomatoes marinate in garlicky olive oil scented with fresh bay leaves. See page 17 for information about this cheese. Provolone cheese can be substituted for Halloumi. If using provolone, grill for only 1 minute.

24 small skewers
$1/4$ cup extra virgin olive oil
3 cloves garlic, pressed
24 fresh bay leaves
24 cherry tomatoes
$1/2$ lb. Halloumi cheese, cut into 24 slices

Soak skewers in warm water for 30 minutes. In a deep bowl, mix oil with garlic. Carefully add bay leaves, tomatoes and cheese, coating pieces well. Marinate at room temperature for 20 minutes. Reserve marinade. On a work surface, thread skewers, alternating cheese, bay leaf and tomato. Cook skewers in the hot grill for 3 minutes. Remove to a serving plate and drizzle with remaining marinade.

SPICY EGGPLANT ROUNDS

Japanese eggplant are ideal for cooking on a contact grill because of their slender size and gentle flavor. Cut into rounds and simply seasoned, they make an ideal accompaniment to grilled entrées or, layered with a spicy filling, they become a zesty appetizer.

olive oil spray
1/4 cup olive oil
1 clove garlic, pressed
1/4 cup pitted oil-cured olives
1/4 cup sun-dried tomato pieces

1/2 cup fresh oregano leaves
1/4 cup freshly grated Romano cheese
1 tsp. red pepper flakes
3 Japanese eggplant, cut horizontally
   into 1/2-inch slices

Spray the cold grill with olive oil and heat for 10 minutes. In a food processor workbowl, combine oil, garlic, olives, tomatoes, oregano, cheese and red pepper flakes. Pulse several times to blend. Mixture should have texture. Make "sandwiches" with eggplant rounds, spreading olive mixture between 2 slices. Arrange on waxed paper on a baking sheet and spray both sides with oil. Place eggplant slices in hot grill and cook for 5 minutes or until grill marks appear and eggplant is tender. Do not overcook or eggplant will be mushy. Serve hot.

STUFFED LEEKS
WITH GINGER DIPPING SAUCE

This elegant appetizer with Pacific Rim flavors is a snap to put together. Select small tender leeks and wash well to rid them of sand.

1 cup commercially prepared mango chutney
$1/4$ cup shredded coconut
$1/4$ cup chopped salted peanuts
$1/2$ tsp. red pepper flakes
1 tbs. finely chopped fresh ginger
2 tbs. chopped fresh cilantro leaves
6 small leeks
fresh cilantro sprigs for garnish
Ginger Dipping Sauce, follows

Spoon chutney into a medium bowl. Using kitchen scissors, cut large pieces into a dice. Add coconut, peanuts, red pepper flakes, ginger and cilantro. Mix well and set aside. Prepare leeks: remove and discard $1/3$ of the green tops and trim root end. Split down the middle almost to root end. Rinse well under running water. In a large saucepan of boiling water, cook leeks until tender. Cool in ice water and remove 4 layers from each leek. Reserve core for another use. Flatten each layer and spread with a portion of the coconut mixture. Roll toward green tops. Grill in batches for 2 to 3 minutes. Garnish with cilantro and serve with *Ginger Dipping Sauce.*

GINGER DIPPING SAUCE

Makes ³/₄ cup

Mirin wine is a low-alcohol sweet wine made from rice. It is available in Japanese markets and in the gourmet foods section of most supermarkets.

¹/₂ cup soy sauce
1 tbs. honey
2 tbs. minced fresh ginger
¹/₄ cup mirin rice wine
1 tbs. peanut oil
2 cloves garlic, minced

In a small serving bowl, combine all ingredients.

COCONUT SHRIMP

Bathing foods in aromatic marinades adds flavor and succulence while protecting them from heat. Here extra-large shrimp steep in a fragrant Thai-inspired marinade and are served with toasted coconut and roasted peanuts, intensifying the flavor.

1/2 cup coconut milk
2 tsp. fish sauce
1 tsp. lime juice
2 tbs. mango chutney
1/2 tsp. curry powder
2 tsp. sweet green chili sauce

16 extra-large shrimp, peeled and
   deveined
olive oil spray
1/2 cup shredded coconut, freshly
   toasted
1/4 cup chopped freshly roasted
   peanuts

In a blender container, combine coconut milk, fish sauce, lime juice, chutney, curry powder and chili sauce. Puree. Pour into a plastic bag and add shrimp. Seal and shake bag to coat shrimp with marinade. Refrigerate for 10 minutes.

When ready, mist the cold grill with olive oil and heat for 10 minutes. Bring shrimp to room temperature and grill for 3 minutes. Remove to a serving dish and sprinkle with coconut and peanuts.

BABY OCTOPUS OREGANO

An easy appetizer to keep guests happy is this summertime favorite from the Greek Isles. It is ready in minutes thanks to the efficiency of the indoor grill. See page 94 for more about buying and cooking octopus.

1/4 cup extra virgin olive oil
3 cloves garlic, pressed
2 tbs. dried oregano
1/2 tsp. sea salt

several grindings black pepper
1 lb. baby octopus
1 loaf French baguette, cut into slices
lemon wedges, optional

In a deep bowl, mix oil, garlic, oregano, salt and pepper. Set aside. Rinse octopus under cold water and pat dry with paper towels. Snip tentacles from heads with scissors. Cut both tentacles and heads into two lengthwise pieces and place in oil mixture. Marinate for 30 minutes. Lift from marinade and quickly cook on the hot grill for no more than 2 minutes. Octopus will become bright white and opaque. Remove to a serving bowl.

While octopus is cooking, microwave reserved marinade on full power for 45 seconds or until bubbly, and pour over grilled octopus. Spoon octopus and marinade over baguette slices and enjoy with or without a squeeze of lemon.

SPICY COCKTAIL KABOBS

A touch of curry belies the Mediterranean origin of these spicy kabobs. They make a good summertime nibble with a cold beer.

24 small wooden skewers
3 tbs. olive oil
1 tsp. lemon juice
1 clove garlic, pressed
$1/2$ tsp. ground coriander
$1/2$ tsp. dried oregano
1 tsp. curry powder

$1/2$ tsp. ground cloves
1 tsp. salt
1 lb. lean pork or lamb, cut into small
   cubes
large fresh oregano leaves
olive oil spray

Soak skewers in warm water for 30 minutes. In a small shallow dish, whisk oil with lemon juice. Add garlic, coriander, oregano, curry powder, cloves and salt. Mix well. Skewer 3 or 4 cubes of meat, alternating with oregano leaves. Place in marinade, turning to coat well. Marinate at room temperature for 30 minutes to 1 hour.

When ready, mist the cold grill with oil and heat for 15 minutes. Cook kabobs for 3 minutes.

TOFU WITH ROSEMARY

For a Mediterranean touch, marinate tofu in a mellow rosemary balsamic vinaigrette.

12 oz. firm tofu
6 tbs. fruit-flavored olive oil
2 tbs. balsamic vinegar
2 tbs. chopped fresh rosemary leaves
coarse salt and freshly ground pepper to taste
olive oil spray
4 tomatoes, thinly sliced
grilled French bread slices

Blot tofu with paper towels to remove excess liquid and cut into 1-inch-thick slices. In a sturdy plastic bag, mix oil, vinegar, rosemary, salt and pepper. Carefully place tofu in marinade, seal and refrigerate overnight.

When ready, mist the grill with olive oil and heat for 10 minutes. Lift tofu from vinaigrette, brush off rosemary leaves and grill tofu for 2 minutes. Reserve vinaigrette. Line a serving platter with tomato slices and place grilled tofu on tomatoes. Spoon reserved vinaigrette over tofu, sprinkle with additional salt and pepper and serve with grilled bread.

BOURBON TOFU FINGERS

This spicy appetizer combines eastern and western flavors that even carnivores will enjoy.

12 small wooden skewers, soaked in
　water for 20 minutes
12 oz. firm tofu
1/4 cup commercially prepared citrus
　vinaigrette
3 tbs. Dijon mustard
3 tbs. bourbon whiskey

1/4 cup orange juice
1/4 cup minced green onions
1/2 tsp. red pepper flakes
1/2 cup sesame seeds
fresh cilantro sprigs
packaged sesame crackers

Following instructions in *Tofu with Rosemary*, page 25, remove excess water from tofu and cut into 1-inch-thick fingers. In a sturdy plastic bag, mix vinaigrette, mustard, whiskey, orange juice, onions and red pepper flakes. Add tofu, seal bag and refrigerate overnight. When ready, mist the cold grill with olive oil and heat for 10 minutes. Spread sesame seeds on a work surface. Lift tofu slices from marinade and remove onion bits. Thread tofu fingers on skewers and coat with sesame seeds. Grill in batches for 2 minutes or until seeds brown. Place on a bed of cilantro sprigs and serve with sesame crackers. For more intense flavor, reserve marinade, microwave on full power for 1 minute and use as a dipping sauce for tofu.

HERBED RICE CAKES

Leftover rice stars in this easy-to-put-together, great-tasting hot hors d'oeuvre.

1 cup cooked rice
1 tsp. pressed garlic
1 tsp. chopped fresh ginger
1 green onion, chopped
3/4 cup minced fresh herbs: basil, tarragon, parsley, mint
1 large egg, beaten
1 cup shredded provolone cheese
1 cup flour
salt and white pepper to taste
olive oil spray

In a large bowl, mix rice, garlic, ginger, green onion, herbs, egg, cheese, flour, salt and pepper. Shape into 1-inch-thick cakes, 2 inches in diameter. Cover and refrigerate for 15 minutes. Mist the cold grill with olive oil and heat while cakes are chilling. When ready, spray cakes with oil and cook in hot grill for 10 minutes.

MEAT DISHES

STEAK FLORENCE-STYLE

Perhaps the simplest way to prepare a T-bone steak is the most satisfying. Seasoning the steak with salt and pepper before grilling produces a crisp, flavorful crust and a succulent interior.

2 tbs. extra virgin olive oil
2 T-bone steaks, 1 inch thick, about 1¼ lb. each
coarse sea salt and freshly ground black pepper to taste
4 lemon wedges

Brush the cold grill with 1 tbs. of the oil and heat for 15 minutes. Trim all fat from steaks and sprinkle both sides with salt and pepper. Grill steaks for 2 to 5 minutes: 2 minutes for rare; 3 to 4 minutes for medium; or 5 minutes for well done. Remove to a warm serving platter. Drizzle remaining 1 tbs. oil over each steak. Wait several minutes before cutting into serving pieces. Remove accumulated juices from the drip pan, spoon some over each serving and garnish with lemon wedges.

SESAME STEAK SKEWERS

Round steak is a good choice for marinades since its firm texture softens as it absorbs the flavors of the marinades. Here Asian flavors permeate the meat.

½ cup soy sauce
2 tbs. sesame oil
2 tbs. rice vinegar
2 tbs. mirin rice wine
2 tbs. honey
¼ cup chopped green onions
2 tbs. minced fresh ginger

¼ cup whole fresh cilantro leaves
¼ cup sesame seeds, toasted
1½ lb. round steak, cut into
  ½-inch-thick slices
16 wooden skewers, soaked in water
  for 30 minutes

In a large plastic bag, mix soy, sesame oil, vinegar, mirin, honey, onions, ginger, 2 tbs. of the cilantro and 2 tbs. of the sesame seeds. Add steak strips. Refrigerate overnight. When ready to grill, bring to room temperature. Drain marinade and discard. Blot excess marinade from steak strips and thread on skewers. Grill in the preheated grill for 3 minutes. Remove to a serving plate and garnish with remaining 2 tbs. cilantro and sesame seeds.

Note: Mirin wine is a sweet rice wine used in cooking. It can be purchased in Asian markets or in the gourmet foods section of many supermakets. Bourbon whiskey can be substituted for mirin if it is not available.

SPANISH-STYLE STEAK STRIPS WITH RED PEPPER RELISH

Servings: 4

Pimenton, a powdered, somewhat smoky-flavored, sweet Spanish paprika, is even better than regular paprika in this dish, if you can find it. Look for it in specialty food stores.

1/4 cup extra virgin olive oil
1 tbs. sherry vinegar
1/2 cup dry sherry
2 cloves garlic, pressed
3 tbs. chopped fresh sage leaves
2 tsp. paprika or pimenton

1 1/2 tsp. sea salt
1/2 tsp. white pepper
1 1/2 lb. round steak, cut into 1/2-inch-thick slices
Red Pepper Relish, follows

In a large plastic bag, mix oil, vinegar, sherry, garlic, sage, paprika, salt and pepper. Add steak strips, seal and knead bag to distribute ingredients over steak. Marinate in the refrigerator overnight.

Bring to room temperature, drain marinade and discard. Wipe excess marinade from steak. Grill in the preheated grill for 3 to 4 minutes. Serve with *Red Pepper Relish*.

RED PEPPER RELISH

1/2 cup diced red bell pepper
1/2 cup diced onion
1/2 tsp. paprika or pimenton
2 tbs. chopped pimiento olives
1 tsp. sherry vinegar
2 tbs. extra virgin olive oil
1/4 cup chopped fresh flat-leaf parsley

In a small bowl, combine all ingredients. Pour directly on the hot grill and cook for 2 minutes. Lift into a serving bowl with a spatula.

LONDON BROIL WITH GREEN SALSA

South of the border spices flavor this family steak. The mild heat is tempered even more by the fresh, tangy green salsa.

2 tbs. minced garlic
1 tsp. sea salt
2 tsp. ground cumin
2 tsp. ground dried oregano
1 tsp. chili powder
2 tbs. wine vinegar
1 1/2 lb. London broil steak (*flank steak*)
Green Salsa, follows

In a small bowl, combine garlic, salt, cumin, oregano, chili powder and vinegar. Mix well and spread on both sides of steak. Refrigerate for 4 hours. Bring to room temperature and cook in the hot grill for 4 to 6 minutes. Let the meat stand for several minutes before carving against the grain. Serve with *Green Salsa*.

GREEN SALSA

1/4 cup chopped onion
1 clove garlic, minced
1/4 cup diced cucumber
1/4 cup diced green bell pepper
1/2 cup diced avocado
1 tomatillo, husk removed and diced
1/2 cup fresh cilantro leaves
1/4 cup tequila
2 tsp. lime juice

Combine ingredients in a small bowl and serve with *London Broil.*

FAJITAS WITH GRILLED SALSA

Always popular with the younger crowd, these south-of-the-border wraps are a cinch to prepare in the indoor grill. Add diced avocado and additional chopped cilantro leaves to commercially prepared tomato salsa if you are in a rush.

1 skirt steak, about 1 1/4 lb.
1 cup beer
2 cloves garlic, minced
1 small onion, thinly sliced
2 tsp. mesquite smoke seasoning
1 tsp. salt
olive oil spray
2 tbs. olive oil
2 tsp. lime juice
1 1/2 cups diced mixed red and yellow bell pepper
1 cup diced tomato
1/2 cup diced firm avocado
1/2 cup chopped green onions
1 small jalapeño pepper, seeded, ribs removed and diced
1/2 cup chopped fresh cilantro leaves
10 flour tortillas

Cut steak into 2 strips to fit the grill. In a plastic bag, mix beer, garlic, onion, smoke seasoning and salt. Add steak strips, coat with marinade, seal bag and refrigerate for 6 hours or overnight. Bring to room temperature before grilling.

Mist the cold grill with olive oil and heat for 15 minutes. In a bowl, whisk together oil and lime juice. Fold in peppers, tomatoes, avocados, onions, jalapeño and cilantro leaves. Set aside.

Heat oven to 200.° Wrap tortillas in foil and warm in oven. Cook steak in hot grill for 2 minutes for medium rare. Place on a cutting board and let stand for 2 minutes. Spoon salsa on hot grill and cook for 3 minutes. Carve steak against the grain into 1/4-inch slices. Serve with warm tortillas and salsa, hot from the grill.

TERIYAKI STEAK STRIPS

Servings: 4–6

These flavorful steak strips can be the base for several other meals, so double the recipe when you have time to grill. Try them with rice, with Grilled Won Ton Wrappers, *page 10, or with* Teriyaki, Broccoli and Peanut Salad, *page 39.*

1 cup soy sauce
2 cups water
½ cup brown sugar, packed
2 cloves garlic, pressed
2-inch slice fresh ginger, pressed

8 fresh cilantro sprigs including stems
1 lb. top sirloin steak
12 wooden skewers, soaked in water
   for 30 minutes
olive oil spray

In a shallow baking dish, whisk together soy sauce, water and brown sugar until sugar dissolves. Add garlic, ginger and 4 of the cilantro sprigs. Set aside. Wipe steak with paper towels and remove all visible fat. Cut steak across the grain into ¼-inch-thick strips and thread on skewers. Marinate skewers in reserved teriyaki mixture for 1 hour at room temperature or overnight in the refrigerator.

Mist the cold grill with oil and heat for 15 minutes. Remove skewers from marinade, blot with paper towels, remove any solid bits and grill for 2 minutes. Garnish with remaining cilantro and serve immediately.

TERIYAKI, BROCCOLI AND PEANUT SALAD

This satisfying salad uses leftover Teriyaki Steak Strips, *page 38, as its base. Combined with crisp broccoli, cherry tomatoes, brown mushrooms, sprouts and crunchy peanuts in a sesame oil vinaigrette, it is perfect for a light summer dinner.*

2 tbs. sesame seeds
1/4 cup peanut oil
1 tsp. sesame oil
3 tbs. rice vinegar
1 tbs. soy sauce
1 tsp. sugar
4 cups broccoli florets

1 cup cherry tomatoes
2 cups small whole brown mushrooms
1/4 cup chopped cilantro leaves
1/4 cup fresh alfalfa sprouts
1/3 cup dry-roasted peanuts
6 skewers grilled *Teriyaki Steak Strips*

In a small skillet over medium heat, toast sesame seeds until fragrant and beginning to brown. Remove from skillet and cool. In a large bowl, whisk together oils, vinegar, soy sauce and sugar until sugar dissolves. Add sesame seeds, broccoli, tomatoes, mushrooms and cilantro to vinaigrette. Mix well and set aside.

Remove skewers from steak strips. Using utility scissors, cut strips 1/4-inch wide. Fold into salad and mix well. Scatter peanuts and sprouts over salad and serve immediately.

SIRLOIN STEAK OVER SPINACH SALAD

Baby spinach salad, spiced with toasted mustard seeds, is the base for rare slices of succulent sirloin steak. Warm French bread and a fruity red wine complete the meal.

2 tsp. mustard seeds
1 1/2 lb. sirloin steak, 1 inch thick
salt and black pepper to taste
1/4 cup plus 1 tbs. olive oil
2 tbs. balsamic vinegar

1 clove garlic, pressed
8 cups baby spinach leaves, loosely packed
2 cups sliced brown mushrooms
1/2 cup crumbled Gorgonzola cheese

In a small sauté pan over medium heat, toast mustard seeds until fragrant. Remove seeds from pan and cool. Heat the grill for 10 minutes. Trim fat from steak and season with salt and pepper. With a teaspoon, drizzle 1 tbs. of the oil evenly over both sides of steak. Spread oil with spoon to cover surfaces. Cook in hot grill for 2 minutes. Meat will be rare. Remove from grill and let stand for 5 minutes before slicing.

In a large salad bowl, whisk remaining 1/4 cup oil, balsamic vinegar, garlic, mustard seeds, salt and pepper. Toss spinach and mushrooms in dressing. Arrange salad on 4 large platters. Slice steak in diagonal slices and arrange over salad. Top with cheese and serve immediately.

SICILIAN-STYLE STEAK

No one would know this savory, crusted steak takes less than 15 minutes to prepare. Serve with Mixed Pepper Grill, *page 128, and* Tomatoes with Herbs, *page 127, for an effortless taste of Southern Italy.*

1 cup seasoned Italian breadcrumbs
$1/3$ cup freshly grated Parmesan cheese
2 tsp. dried oregano
1 tsp. salt
$1/2$ tsp. freshly ground black pepper
$1/4$ cup olive oil
6 small steaks, $1/2$-inch thick

In a shallow utility pan, mix breadcrumbs, cheese, oregano, salt, pepper and 3 tbs. of the oil. Microwave, uncovered, on full power for 1 minute. Fluff with a fork and set aside. Heat the grill for 15 minutes. When ready, brush steaks with remaining 3 tbs. oil and grill for 3 to 5 minutes, to desired doneness. Remove from grill and roll in reserved breadcrumb mixture, coating each steak with crumbs. Serve immediately.

BEEF SCALOPPINE WITH TARRAGON

The delicate, spicy-sweet taste of tarragon marries well with thinly sliced beef scallops. A splash of Madeira—poured directly into the grill and spooned over the beef—adds dimension to the dish.

1/4 cup extra virgin olive oil
2 large sprigs fresh tarragon
salt and freshly ground black pepper
1/4 cup Madeira wine
1 1/4 lb. thinly sliced beef scallops
2 tbs. chopped fresh tarragon for garnish

In a plastic bag, mix oil, sprigs of tarragon, salt, pepper and 2 tbs. of the wine. Add scallops and coat well with mixture. Seal bag and refrigerate for several hours or overnight. When ready, lift scallops from marinade, blot with paper towels and cook in the hot grill for no longer than 1 minute. Remove to a warm serving platter. Spoon remaining 2 tbs. wine into grill, catching juices in the drip pan. Pour over scallops and scatter tarragon over top. Serve immediately.

SWISS BURGERS

Baby Swiss cheese has a more delicate flavor than regular Swiss cheese. Use regular Swiss if baby Swiss is not available.

olive oil spray
1 1/2 lb. ground round beef steak
1 tsp. Worcestershire sauce
2 tsp. honey mustard
coarse salt and freshly ground pepper to taste
2 oz. baby Swiss cheese, cut into six 2-x-2-x-1/4-inch slices
6 seeded Kaiser rolls, lightly spread with mustard

Mist the cold grill with olive oil and heat for 15 minutes. In a medium bowl, mix ground beef, Worcestershire sauce, mustard, salt and pepper. Shape into 6 patties with 1 slice cheese buried in the middle of each. Cook in grill for 2 to 4 minutes. Slide into prepared rolls. Place sandwiches back on grill and warm for 1 minute.

PACIFIC RIM BURGERS WITH SHAVED CHINESE CABBAGE

Servings: 4

The exotic, complex flavor of the burgers is in contrast to the clean, tart taste of the razor-thin cabbage.

olive oil spray
1 lb. ground round beef steak
2 tbs. hoisin sauce
1 tbs. dry sherry
1 tbs. sesame oil
2 tbs. soy sauce

1 tsp. Chinese 5-spice powder
1 tsp. grated fresh ginger
1 clove garlic, minced
1 tbs. chopped fresh cilantro
Shaved Chinese Cabbage, follows

Mist the cold grill with olive oil and heat for 15 minutes. In a large bowl, mix ground beef, sherry, oil, soy sauce, 5-spice powder, ginger, garlic and cilantro. Shape into 4 patties. Grill patties for 2 to 4 minutes. Serve immediately with *Shaved Chinese Cabbage.*

SHAVED CHINESE CABBAGE

6 cups shaved cabbage
3 tbs. peanut oil
1 tsp. sesame oil
3 tbs. rice vinegar
$\frac{1}{2}$ tsp. soy sauce
$\frac{1}{4}$ cup almonds, toasted
2 tbs. sesame seeds, toasted
$\frac{1}{4}$ cup cilantro leaves

Shave cabbage: On a work surface, cut cabbage in half. Hold cabbage at a 10° angle with stem side up, cut side out. Shred cabbage by "shaving" cut side with a sharp knife.

In a large serving bowl, whisk oils, vinegar and soy sauce. Add cabbage and coat with dressing. Top with almonds, sesame seeds and cilantro.

DOUBLE CHEESE BURGERS

Sharp cheddar cheese melts in the middle of the burger in the grill, and on the top of the burger when placed in a warm oven. Hickory Liquid Smoke provides the woodsy flavor.

olive oil spray
1 1/2 lb. ground round beef steak
3–5 tsp. hickory Liquid Smoke
salt and pepper to taste
1/4 lb. sharp cheddar cheese, cut into 12 thin slices
6 large hamburger buns

Mist the cold grill with olive oil and heat for 15 minutes. Also heat oven to 350.° In a medium bowl, mix ground beef, Liquid Smoke, salt and pepper. Shape into 6 patties with 1 slice of the cheese buried in the middle of each. Cook in grill for 2 to 4 minutes. Slide grilled burgers into bottom halves of buns, top with remaining cheese and place on a foil-lined baking sheet. Bake until cheese topping melts. Cover with bun tops and serve immediately.

MIDDLE EASTERN BURGERS
WITH GRILLED WRAPPERS

Servings: 4

This burger works well with either ground beef or ground lamb. Select leaner cuts like ground beef round or ground lamb leg slices to hold the fat in check. The crisp wrappers are a novelty "cover" for the burgers, but grilled pita bread is more traditional.

24 round won ton wrappers
1 lb. ground lamb
1/3 cup finely chopped onions
1/4 tsp. ground allspice
1/4 tsp. ground cumin
1/4 tsp. cinnamon

1/2 tsp. ground coriander
1/2 tsp. freshly ground black pepper
1/4 cup finely chopped walnuts
1 tsp. chopped fresh flat-leaf parsley
green onions, sliced radish and
    additional parsley for garnish

Grill wrappers in batches for 4 minutes until crisp and slightly tan. Remove and set aside. In a large bowl, mix all ingredients except garnish. Form into patties and grill for 4 to 6 minutes. Garnish with onions, radish slices and parsley. Serve with grilled wrappers.

LEMON VEAL WITH PARSLEY-CAPER SAUCE

Breast of veal, trimmed of fat, cut into riblets and marinated in a lemon-wine sauce produces an upscale yet economical adult entrée. Serve with steamed rice and a green salad.

1 cup chopped onion
4 cloves garlic, pressed
$1/4$ cup chopped fresh flat-leaf parsley, packed
$1/4$ cup dry white wine
$1/2$ cup lemon juice
1 tbs. grated lemon zest
1 tbs. dried oregano
$31/2$ lb. shoulder of veal, cut into riblets and trimmed of fat
Parsley-Caper Sauce, follows

In a heavy-duty plastic bag, combine all ingredients. Seal bag and manipulate ingredients to saturate veal. Refrigerate overnight. Bring to room temperature before cooking in the hot grill for 10 minutes. Serve with *Parsley-Caper Sauce.*

PARSLEY-CAPER SAUCE

Tangy and tart, yet rich and smooth, this sauce is excellent with other grilled meats and fish.

1 cup chopped fresh flat-leaf parsley, packed
3 cloves garlic, minced
2 tbs. capers, rinsed and drained
2 tsp. grated lemon zest
1/2 cup white wine
1/4 cup extra virgin olive oil

In a 4-cup microwave-safe pitcher, combine all ingredients. Mix well and microwave on full power for 3 minutes. Stir and serve warm.

GRILLED VEAL ROLL-UPS (SALTIMBOCCA)

Servings: 4

The popular veal roll-ups with prosciutto and provolone are cooked in the contact grill in half the time of the traditional sautéed method. Excellent company fare with none of the bother!

8 slices veal scallops
salt and white pepper to taste
8 slices prosciutto
8 slices provolone cheese
olive oil spray
1/4 cup Marsala wine

Between two sheets of plastic wrap, lightly pound veal scallops to 1/4-inch thickness with a meat mallet. Salt and pepper each scallop and stack with 1 slice each prosciutto and provolone cheese. Roll and secure ends with toothpicks. Mist the cold grill with olive oil and heat for 15 minutes. Spray saltimbocca on both sides with oil and grill for 1 1/2 minutes. Remove to a warm serving plate. Spoon wine over hot grill, catching juices in the drip pan. Pour wine juices over saltimbocca and serve immediately.

FENNEL-CRUSTED PORK CHOPS

A light coating of crushed fennel seeds adds a textured, flavorful zest to the chops.

1 tsp. fennel seeds
1 tbs. garlic powder
1 tsp. kosher salt
$1/8$ tsp. white pepper
olive oil spray
8 pork chops, $1/2$-inch thick

In a spice or coffee grinder, coarsely grind fennel seeds. In a small bowl, mix ground fennel with garlic powder, salt and pepper. Spray both sides of pork chops with olive oil. Spread chops with fennel mixture. Heat the grill for 5 minutes. Grill chops for 4 minutes, or until grill marks appear and meat is no longer pink.

SAGE-STUFFED PORK ROLLS

Double sage flavors come to the fore in this easy-to-prepare grilled entrée. Serve with commercially prepared cranberry sauce or a fruity chutney.

1 tsp. dried sage
1 tbs. minced garlic
$1/4$ cup minced fresh sage leaves
$1/4$ cup grated Parmesan cheese
1 tsp. salt
$1/8$ tsp. white pepper
1 tbs. extra virgin olive oil
8 pork chops, $1/2$-inch thick
olive oil spray

In a small bowl, mix dried sage with garlic, fresh sage, cheese, salt and pepper. Set aside. Place chops between two sheets of plastic wrap. With a meat mallet, pound chops to $1/8$-inch thick. Place 1 chop on plastic wrap and spread with $1/2$ tsp. sage mixture. Roll chop, forming a cylinder. Continue procedure until all chops are stuffed and rolled. Mist the cold grill with olive oil and heat for 10 minutes. Grill chops for 5 minutes or until cooked through.

PORK MARSALA

Boneless pork loin adapts well to almost any type of seasoning. The heady Marsala marinade infuses the loin with a nutty, semi-sweet flavor.

$1/4$ cup dry Marsala wine
2 tbs. extra virgin olive oil
$1/2$ tsp. cinnamon
1 tsp. garlic powder
$1/8$ tsp. white pepper
8 pork loin chops, $1/2$-inch thick

Combine Marsala, olive oil, cinnamon, garlic powder and pepper in a small bowl or plastic bag. Add pork chops and marinate in the refrigerator for 8 hours or overnight. Remove from refrigerator 30 minutes before grilling. Blot excess marinade with a paper towel. Grill chops in the preheated grill for 5 minutes, or until cooked through.

SPICY PORK CHOPS

World travel has broadened the palate as well as the mind as people are seeking to re-create the exotic tastes they may have experienced abroad. Boneless pork chops take on the flavor of the Levant with this unusual spice rub.

1 tbs. ground allspice
2 tsp. cinnamon
1 tsp. ground cardamom
1 tbs. ground nutmeg
1 tsp. salt
2 tsp. freshly ground black pepper
8 pork loin chops, $1/2$-inch thick
olive oil spray

In a small bowl, combine allspice, cinnamon, cardamom, nutmeg, salt and peppercorns. Coat chops with spice rub and set aside for 30 minutes. Spray the cold grill with olive oil and heat for 10 minutes. Grill chops for 4 minutes. Serve immediately.

BUTTERFLIED PORK TENDERLOIN

Purchasing a small whole pork loin tenderloin is the economical way to serve tender pork entrées. It may be cut into chops and small roasts and frozen for later use.

1 tbs. olive oil
1 tbs. Dijon mustard
$1/4$ cup dry white wine
$1/2$ cup chopped onions
3 cloves garlic, minced
1 cup chopped fresh tarragon
2 tbs. coarsely ground black pepper
1 lb. center-cut pork loin roast

In a small bowl, whisk together olive oil, Dijon mustard and wine. Pour into a large plastic bag. Add onions, garlic, tarragon and black pepper. Mix well and set aside. Carefully cut through center of pork loin, stopping $1/2$-inch from other side. Spread loin apart and place in marinade, distributing vegetables around it. Seal bag and refrigerate overnight. Bring to room temperature. Remove loin and wipe away any residue of marinade. Cook in the hot grill for 12 minutes or until loin is cooked through. Remove from grill and let stand for 5 minutes before carving.

DOWN SOUTH PORK KABOBS

Servings: 8

Since meats cook so quickly in the indoor grill, it is necessary to parboil or blanch some vegetables before grilling. Do not mix vegetables when blanching. To blanch: In a medium saucepan, bring 8 cups water to a boil. Add vegetable and boil until crisp-tender. Drain quickly and refresh with cold water.

$1/3$ cup commercially prepared barbecue sauce
$1/2$ cup bourbon whiskey or apple juice
1 tbs. chopped fresh flat-leaf parsley
1 tsp. chopped fresh thyme leaves
$1\frac{1}{2}$ lb. boneless pork loin, cut into $1\frac{1}{2}$-inch cubes
16 cherry tomatoes
16 slices green bell pepper, blanched
16 small white onions, blanched
16 wooden skewers

In a large plastic bag, combine barbecue sauce, whiskey, parsley and thyme. Place pork in marinade and refrigerate for 8 hours or overnight. Remove from refrigerator 30 minutes before cooking. Soak 16 wooden skewers in water for at least 30 minutes. Thread skewers, alternating pork with vegetables. Cook kabobs in batches in the hot grill for 4 minutes. Serve on skewers.

BURGUNDY LAMB STEAKS

Because of the bones, shoulder or rib lamb chops do not cook evenly in the contact grill. The sirloin, cut from the meaty leg with only a small round bone, does quite well. For lamb lovers, it is economical to purchase the entire leg of lamb and have it cut into 3/4-inch slices. The tender center cuts are prepared like chops, while the end pieces are marinated and used for kabobs or ground for burgers.

1/4 cup extra virgin olive oil
1/2 cup Burgundy wine
1 tbs. dried tarragon
salt and freshly ground pepper
4 lamb sirloin steaks, 3/4-inch thick
olive oil spray

In a large plastic bag, mix oil, wine, tarragon, salt and pepper. Add lamb, mix well and refrigerate overnight. When ready, mist the cold grill with olive oil and heat for 15 minutes. Lift lamb from marinade and grill for 2 to 4 minutes, or to preferred degree of doneness.

LAMB WITH BLACK OLIVES

Lamb steaks are simply grilled and served with chopped black olives flavored with fresh oregano and lemon juice.

1/4 cup extra virgin olive oil
1 tbs. lemon juice
2 tbs. chopped fresh oregano leaves
1 pinch red pepper flakes
1/2 cup chopped kalamata olives
4 lamb steaks, 3/4-inch thick
salt and pepper to taste

In a small bowl, mix 2 tbs. of the oil, lemon juice, oregano, red pepper flakes and olives. Set aside. Heat the grill for 15 minutes. Place steaks on waxed paper, brush with remaining 2 tbs. oil and season with salt and pepper. When ready, grill for 3 to 5 minutes and serve with olive sauce.

ARMENIAN LAMB KABOBS

Sun-dried tomatoes packed in oil provide a colorful as well as tangy counterpoint to these spicy lamb kabobs. Serve with instant couscous, prepared according to package directions but flavored with lemon zest and chopped fresh mint. A fresh tomato salad, accented with sun-dried tomato bits, thinly sliced lemons and zesty cilantro, provides a tangy accent.

6 tbs. extra virgin olive oil
1/4 cup lemon juice
6 cloves garlic, pressed
1 tsp. ground ginger
1 tsp. ground coriander
1 tsp. curry powder
salt and pepper to taste

1 lb. lamb, cut into 2-inch cubes
1 cup oil-packed sun-dried whole
   tomatoes, drained
16 large mint leaves
8 wooden skewers, soaked in water for
   20 minutes

In a large plastic bag, mix 1/4 cup of the oil, lemon juice, garlic, ginger, coriander, curry powder, salt and pepper. Add lamb, coat with mixture, seal bag and refrigerate for 6 hours or overnight.

Bring lamb to room temperature. Brush the cold grill with remaining 2 tbs. oil and heat for 15 minutes. Lift lamb from marinade and thread with tomatoes and mint. Grill kabobs for 2 to 3 minutes.

SWEET SAUSAGE OVER JASMINE RICE

Sausage, marinated with red onions and dried figs in a balsamic vinaigrette, makes an unusual topping for lemon-parsley jasmine rice. Crispy flat bread and fragrant, hot tea complete the meal.

1/4 cup extra virgin olive oil
3 tbs. balsamic vinegar
2 cloves garlic, minced
2 tbs. chopped fresh flat-leaf parsley
6 sweet sausage links
2 medium red onions, sliced 1/4-inch thick
8 dried Turkish figs, cut in half
Jasmine Rice, follows

In a small bowl, whisk oil, vinegar, garlic and parsley. Pour into a plastic bag. Add sausage, onion and figs, coating them with vinaigrette. Marinate in the refrigerator for 1 hour.

When ready to grill, bring to room temperature and lift from marinade. Cook in the hot grill for 3 minutes. Arrange over *Jasmine Rice* and serve immediately.

JASMINE RICE

3 tbs. extra virgin olive oil
2 tbs. chopped lemon zest
2 tbs. chopped fresh flat-leaf parsley
6 cups prepared hot jasmine rice

In a warm serving bowl, whisk oil, zest and parsley. Fold in hot rice and mix well. Serve with grilled sausage and figs.

LAMB HUNTER-STYLE

The aromas of juniper berries, rosemary and bay permeate the lamb, giving it a savory, earthy flavor. The longer the marinade, the stronger the flavor, so choose the time to your personal taste.

1 cup extra virgin olive oil
1 cup Cabernet Sauvignon or other strong red wine
5 cloves garlic, pressed
1 tsp. ground allspice
1 tbs. slightly crushed juniper berries
1/4 cup fresh rosemary leaves
4 large bay leaves, crumbled
1/2 cup fresh mint leaves, packed
sea salt and freshly ground black pepper to taste
4 boneless lamb sirloin steaks, 3/4-inch thick

In a plastic bag, mix ½ cup of the oil, wine, garlic, allspice, juniper berries, rosemary, bay, mint, salt and pepper. Add lamb steaks, coat well and refrigerate for 48 or more hours (up to 4 days), turning bag daily. When ready, remove lamb from marinade, blot with paper towels to remove clinging herbs and bring to room temperature. Brush the cold grill with 1 tbs. of the oil and heat for 15 minutes. Brush steaks with remaining 3 tbs. oil and grill for 2 to 4 minutes.

FISH DISHES

WALNUT-CRUSTED SOLE
WITH HORSERADISH SAUCE

For the fanciers of fillet of sole, this preparation will surely please. The crunchy walnut-crumb coating has a touch of mustard and spice to enhance the delicate sole flavor, while the creamy horseradish sauce provides a smooth finish.

$1/2$ cup walnut pieces
$1/2$ cup French breadcrumbs
2 tsp. minced shallot
2 tsp. finely chopped mixed fresh flat-
   leaf parsley and marjoram
$1/4$ cup walnut oil or mild olive oil
2 tsp. Dijon mustard

4 thick fillets of sole, $1/4$ lb. each
salt and pepper to taste
olive oil spray
lemon wedges and fresh flat-leaf
   parsley sprigs for garnish
Horseradish Sauce, follows

Place walnut pieces in a sturdy plastic bag and crush with a meat mallet to the consistency of coarse breadcrumbs. In a shallow dish, combine walnut crumbs with breadcrumbs, shallot and herbs. Mix well. In a separate shallow dish, whisk together oil and mustard. Salt and pepper sole fillets and moisten both sides of fillets with mustard mixture. If ends of fillets are significantly thinner than middle section, tuck ends under for uniformity. Reserve unused mustard mixture. Heavily coat underside of fillet only with crumb mixture. Place on waxed paper on a baking sheet crumb-side down and refrigerate while making *Horseradish Sauce.*

Bring fillets to room temperature. Mist the cold grill with olive oil. Heat grill for 10 minutes, or until very hot. Lightly brush oiled sides of fillets with reserved mustard mixture. Place fillets in grill crumb-side down and cook for 3 minutes. Remove to serving plates and garnish with lemon slices and parsley. Serve with *Horseradish Sauce.*

HORSERADISH SAUCE

Makes about 1 cup

$1/4$ cup commercially prepared horseradish sauce
$1/3$ cup mayonnaise
1 tbs. Dijon mustard
3 tsp. lemon juice
1 tbs. finely chopped lemon zest
$1/4$ cup mixed minced fresh flat-leaf parsley and marjoram

In a small serving bowl, whisk together horseradish sauce, mayonnaise, mustard, lemon juice and zest until well blended. Fold in mixed herbs.

SEA BASS WITH
GRILLED BELL PEPPER SALSA

Grilled lemony bell pepper salsa tops buttery sea bass fillets for a special sea food entrée. Select sea bass fillets that are no more than 1 inch thick for preparing in a contact grill. Thicker cuts will not cook evenly.

olive oil spray
$1/4$ cup extra virgin olive oil
2 tbs. lemon juice
4 sea bass fillets, $1/4$ lb. each
salt and pepper to taste
1 tbs. finely minced lemon zest
$1 1/4$ cups coarsely chopped red and green bell pepper
1 cup coarsely chopped red onion
1 cup coarsely chopped Roma tomatoes, without juice
$1/2$–1 tsp. hot pepper sauce
$1/2$ cup chopped fresh cilantro leaves

Mist the cold grill with olive oil and heat for 10 minutes. In a shallow dish, mix 2 tbs. of the oil with 1 tbs. of the lemon juice. Salt and pepper both sides of fillets, coat well with oil mixture and marinate while preparing salsa.

In a medium bowl, mix together remaining 2 tbs. oil, 1 tbs. lemon juice, zest, bell peppers, onion, tomatoes, hot pepper sauce and $1/4$ cup of the cilantro. Pour vegetable mixture directly into hot grill. Cook for 3 minutes or until crisp-tender. Scrape into a serving dish and set aside. Wipe down any crispy bits with a paper towel. Close grill and heat again for 5 minutes. Turn sea bass fillets in marinade so both sides are moistened. Cook in hot grill for 5 minutes. Remove to serving plates, sprinkle with remaining $1/4$ cup cilantro and serve with remaining salsa.

SEA BASS WITH CITRUS DRESSING

A tangy citrus dressing mellowed by Marsala wine complements succulent sea bass fillets.

1 tbs. finely chopped orange zest
3 tsp. finely chopped lemon zest
1/4 cup dried currants
1 tbs. finely chopped fresh flat-leaf parsley
1/4 cup Marsala wine
olive oil spray
4 sea bass fillets, 1/2-inch thick
salt and freshly ground pepper
flat-leaf parsley sprigs, orange and lemon slices for garnish

In a small bowl, mix together orange zest, lemon zest, currants, parsley and Marsala. Steep for 30 minutes at room temperature. Mist the cold grill with oil and heat for 15 minutes. Spray sea bass with oil, season with salt and pepper and grill for 2 to 3 minutes. Arrange on a serving plate with citrus dressing spooned over fillets. Garnish with orange, lemon and parsley.

TUNA WITH ARUGULA

The peppery bite of arugula accents the meaty texture of tuna, while the balsamic vinaigrette sweetens the dish.

coarse salt and freshly ground pepper
4 tuna steaks, $1/2$-inch thick, about 6 oz. each
$1/4$ cup plus 2 tbs. extra virgin olive oil
2 cloves garlic, pressed
3 tbs. balsamic vinegar
8 cups fresh arugula leaves

Salt and pepper tuna and brush with 2 tbs. of the oil. Set aside. In a large salad bowl, combine remaining $1/4$ cup oil, garlic and vinegar. Whisk until blended. Add arugula and toss gently.

In the hot grill, cook tuna for 3 to 4 minutes. Place on serving plates with arugula salad to one side. Season with additional salt and pepper, if desired.

LAVENDER-SCENTED TUNA

Unsprayed lavender leaves and flowers lend their perfume to fresh tuna fillets. If lavender is not available, substitute dried herbes de Provence.

2 tbs. finely chopped fresh lavender flowers and leaves, or 1 tbs. herbes de Provence
2 tbs. finely chopped fresh flat-leaf parsley
1 tbs. finely chopped lemon zest
1 tsp. salt

½ tsp. freshly ground pepper
olive oil spray
4 tuna steaks, ¾-inch thick
1 clove garlic, pressed
¼ cup red wine
2 tbs. unsalted butter
fresh lavender sprigs for garnish

In a shallow bowl, mix lavender or herbs de Provence, parsley, zest, salt and pepper. Spray tuna with oil and roll in lavender mixture. Cover bowl and keep tuna at room temperature for 30 minutes while flavors develop.

In a microwave-safe bowl, combine garlic, wine and butter. Microwave uncovered on full power for 1 minute. Set aside. Spray the cold grill with oil and heat for 15 minutes. Grill tuna for 4 minutes. Warm reserved wine sauce in microwave and pour over tuna. Garnish with lavender sprigs.

TUNA BURGERS

These Provençal-flavored tuna burgers are right at home served on warm olive bread.

2 cans (6 oz.) tuna, packed in oil
1 tbs. finely chopped shallots
1 tsp. capers, rinsed and drained
1 tbs. chopped niçoise olives
2 tbs. sun-dried tomato pieces
2 tbs. chopped fresh basil
1 cup seasoned breadcrumbs
salt and freshly ground black pepper
1 egg, slightly beaten
olive oil spray

Drain 2 tbs. oil from tuna and set aside. In a large bowl, combine tuna and remaining oil, shallots, capers, olives, tomatoes, basil, breadcrumbs and salt and pepper. Add egg and mix well. Shape mixture into 4 burgers, ¾-inch thick, and brush with reserved 2 tbs. oil. Spray the cold grill with oil and heat for 10 minutes. Grill burgers for 4 minutes.

MARLIN WITH CUMIN-LIME RUB

Not everyone is fortunate enough to come across marlin fillets, but when they do appear, here is a spicy, fresh tasting preparation that also works well with any firm-fleshed fish, such as sea bass, swordfish, monkfish or shark.

olive oil spray
3 tbs. lime juice
$1/4$ cup olive oil
2 tbs. grated lime zest
1 tbs. ground cumin
$1/4$ tsp. red pepper flakes
salt and pepper to taste
4 marlin fillets, $3/4$-inch thick
lime wedges for garnish

Mist the cold grill with olive oil spray and heat for 5 minutes. In a shallow bowl, whisk together lime juice, olive oil, zest, cumin and red pepper flakes. Salt, pepper and coat fish with lime mixture. Grill fish for 3 minutes or until flesh is opaque. Garnish with lime wedges.

BONELESS TROUT WITH ORANGE ALMOND STUFFING

The mild flavor of trout is enhanced by the tangy citrus nut stuffing. Select small, tender lake trout for this preparation.

1/4 cup chopped toasted almonds
2 tbs. toasted breadcrumbs
2 cloves garlic, pressed
2 tbs. chopped fresh tarragon
2 tbs. orange marmalade, large rinds diced

6 tbs. olive oil
4 small whole boneless trout
salt and freshly ground black pepper to taste
lemon wedges and fresh tarragon sprigs for garnish

In a small bowl, mix together almonds, breadcrumbs, garlic, tarragon, marmalade and 1 tbs. of the oil. Using a paper towel, lightly coat the cold grill with oil and heat for 15 minutes. Blot trout with paper towels. Using a sharp knife, make 3 diagonal cuts on side of each trout. Rub each fish with 1 tbs. oil, salt and pepper. Spoon stuffing into body cavity of each fish. Press together. Grill for 3 to 4 minutes. Carefully remove to a serving platter. Garnish with lemon wedges and tarragon sprigs.

BLACKENED CATFISH FILLETS WITH AIOLI

Louisiana seasoning provides the heat while the aioli smooths the fire. When in a rush, use commercially prepared blackened fish seasoning and add pressed garlic to your favorite mayonnaise.

1 tsp. cayenne pepper
1 tsp. freshly ground black pepper
2 tsp. paprika
1 1/2 tsp. salt
1 tsp. garlic powder
1 tsp. onion powder
1 tsp. dried thyme
1 tsp. dried oregano
4 catfish fillets, 6 oz. each
olive oil spray
Aioli, follows

In a small bowl, mix together cayenne, black pepper, paprika, salt, garlic powder, onion powder, thyme and oregano. Spray catfish with olive oil and coat with seasoning mixture. Mist the cold grill with olive oil spray and heat for 15 minutes. Grill fillets for 4 to 5 minutes. Serve with aioli.

AIOLI

4 cloves garlic, pressed
¼ tsp. salt
2 egg yolks
1¼ cups extra virgin olive oil
1 tbs. lemon juice
⅛ tsp. white pepper

In a food processor workbowl, pulse garlic, salt and egg yolks until well mixed. With processor running, gradually add oil in small drops very slowly, blending well before adding more oil. As aioli starts to thicken, add oil in larger drops. Be sure all oil is incorporated into mixture before adding more oil. When half of the oil is incorporated, add remaining oil in a slow, steady stream. Continue blending until aioli is thick and creamy. Stir in lemon juice and white pepper. Cover leftover aioli tightly and store in the refrigerator for up to 2 days.

GREEN TEA-MARINATED SNAPPER

The healthful properties of green tea date back to 3000 BC when Chinese emperor Shen Nong proclaimed it to be a "health elixir" that warded off disease and improved health. In addition to drinking green tea, chefs have discovered the subtle flavors green tea imparts to foods. Here snapper is simply marinated in green tea with garlic, basil and olive oil and then served with a tea-infused butter. Carry the theme further by steaming white rice in green tea as an accompaniment.

2 tbs. green tea leaves
2 tbs. water
3/4 cup olive oil
1 clove garlic, pressed
1/2 cup chopped fresh basil leaves, packed
salt and freshly ground black pepper
4 red snapper fillets, 6 oz. each
Basil Mint Tea Butter, follows

In a blender container, whirl tea with water to rehydrate. Add oil, garlic, basil, salt and pepper. Puree. Pour marinade into a plastic bag. Add snapper and refrigerate overnight. Bring snapper to room temperature before cooking in the hot grill for 3 to 4 minutes. Serve with basil mint tea butter.

BASIL MINT TEA BUTTER

¼ lb. butter, room temperature
2 tbs. minced green onion
2 tbs. finely chopped fresh basil leaves
1 tbs. finely chopped fresh mint leaves
1 tbs. green tea leaves

In a small bowl, cream butter with onion, basil, mint and tea. On a sheet of plastic wrap, roll butter into a log and refrigerate until firm. Cut log into rounds.

CORNMEAL-CRUSTED CATFISH

This dish shouts, "Southern cooking!" but is low in fat without sacrificing flavor. Serve with cornbread, greens and black-eyed peas.

³/₄ cup low-fat buttermilk
1 ¹/₂ cups cornmeal
2 tsp. Old Bay seasoning or poultry seasoning
salt and white pepper
4 catfish fillets, 6 oz. each
olive oil spray

Pour buttermilk into a wide utility dish. In a plastic bag, combine cornmeal, Old Bay or poultry seasoning, salt and pepper. Blot catfish with a paper towel and moisten with buttermilk. Put into bag with cornmeal mixture and shake until well coated. Refrigerate fillets while heating grill.

Mist the grill with olive oil and heat for 10 minutes. Bring fish to room temperature. Grill for 4 minutes.

SWORDFISH STEAKS
WITH PARSLEY SAUCE

Servings: 4

The rich flavor of swordfish is complemented by this garlicky parsley sauce. A well seasoned fresh tomato salad is a good accompaniment.

2/3 cup plus 2 tbs. extra virgin olive oil
4 cloves garlic, finely minced
2 anchovy fillets, finely chopped
1 cup chopped fresh flat-leaf parsley
3 tbs. finely chopped fresh oregano
coarse salt and freshly ground black pepper to taste
1/4 cup water
4 swordfish steaks, 1/2-inch thick
lemon wedges for garnish

Heat the grill for 15 minutes. Salt and pepper swordfish and coat with 2 tbs. of the oil. Set aside. In a small serving bowl, combine remaining 2/3 cup oil, garlic, anchovy, parsley, oregano, salt and pepper. Whisk in water to make a sauce. Grill fish for 2 to 3 minutes and serve with parsley sauce and lemon wedges.

COD WITH TAPENADE

Tapenade is a spicy textured condiment originating in France's Provence region. This savory combination of ripe olives, olive oil, anchovies, capers, lemon and seasoning adds a zest to grilled foods. Plum preserves are added to commercially prepared tapenade for a sweet, tangy dressing for the grilled cod. You can find tapenade in gourmet food markets or you can prepare your own.

3/4 cup *Black Olive Tapenade*, follows
1 tbs. plum preserves
2 tbs. chopped fresh mint
olive oil spray
salt and black pepper to taste
4 cod fillets, 1/2-inch thick
fresh mint leaves for garnish

In a small bowl, combine tapenade with plum preserves and mint. Mix well and set aside. Mist the cold grill with olive oil and heat for 15 minutes. Salt and pepper fillets, spray with oil and cook in hot grill for 4 minutes. Serve with tapenade and mint leaf garnish.

BLACK OLIVE TAPENADE

3/4 cup pitted California black olives
3/4 cup pitted kalamata olives
2 tbs. capers, rinsed
2 anchovy fillets, drained
2 cloves garlic, crushed
2 tbs. grated Parmesan cheese
1/4 cup fresh flat-leaf parsley leaves
2 tbs. sweet Marsala wine
1/4 cup extra virgin olive oil
2 tbs. pine nuts, toasted
freshly ground pepper to taste

With a food processor, process olives, capers, anchovies, garlic, Parmesan, parsley and Marsala until coarsely chopped. With machine running, slowly add oil until mixture is blended but still has some texture. Fold in nuts and pepper. Place in a bowl, cover and refrigerate for 12 hours before using.

JAPANESE-STYLE SALMON

The crunchy fresh vegetables and won ton wrappers must be sliced very thinly so their texture does not overpower the tender flesh of the salmon. Tamari sauce is very similar to soy sauce, with a milder, less salty flavor.

4 salmon fillets, 6 oz. each
1/2 cup plus 1 tbs. tamari, soy or teriyaki sauce
2 won ton wrappers
1/2 cup mirin rice wine
1/4 tsp. red pepper flakes
1 tbs. lime juice
1/2 peeled cucumber, cut into thin strips
4 green onions, cut into thin strips
1/4 cup finely sliced sweet pickled ginger
1/4 cup radish sprouts
1/4 cup chopped fresh cilantro leaves

In a small plastic bag, marinate salmon in $1/2$ cup of the tamari for 15 minutes. Spray cold grill with olive oil and heat for 5 minutes. Slice won ton skins into thin strips and grill for 5 minutes until crisp and slightly brown. Separate strips while still warm and set aside. Keep grill hot. In a microwave-safe bowl, heat wine on full power in a microwave for 2 minutes. Add pepper, lime juice and remaining 1 tbs. tamari. Set aside. Remove salmon from marinade and grill for 4 minutes. Place on a platter. Scatter cucumber, onion, ginger, sprouts, cilantro and won ton slices over salmon. Spoon sauce around perimeter of salmon.

LEMON MUSTARD SALMON

Tangy lemon-mustard-flavored butter melts into the hot, grilled salmon to produce a mouthwatering entrée.

1/4 cup butter, at room temperature
3 tsp. lemon juice
2 tsp. Dijon mustard
1 tsp. finely chopped lemon zest
1 tbs. finely chopped fresh tarragon
olive oil spray
4 salmon fillets, 1/2-inch thick
salt and freshly ground black pepper

In a small bowl, cream butter with lemon juice, mustard, zest and tarragon. On a sheet of plastic wrap, roll butter mixture into a log and refrigerate until firm. Mist the cold grill with olive oil and heat for 15 minutes.

Blot fillets with a paper towel, spray with oil and season with salt and pepper. Grill for 4 minutes. Top with lemon butter and serve hot.

GRILLED SALMON WITH HERB SALAD

The mild taste of salmon lends itself to herbal preparations. Garden herbs dressed with chive oil and raspberry vinegar provide the crunchy side to the delicately flavored salmon.

1/4 cup finely chopped fresh chives
1/4 cup plus 2 tbs. extra virgin olive oil
3 tbs. raspberry vinegar
4 salmon fillets, about 6 oz. each
salt and freshly ground black pepper
1 cup torn garden lettuce leaves

1 cup arugula leaves
1 cup fresh flat-leaf parsley leaves
1/2 cup fresh basil leaves
1/4 cup small fresh mint leaves
1/4 cup fresh marjoram leaves
fresh chives for garnish

In a medium bowl, combine chives and oil. Let stand at room temperature for about 30 minutes. When ready, add vinegar to chive oil. Salt and pepper salmon and coat both sides with 2 tbs. of the flavored oil. Set aside. Heat the grill for 10 minutes. In a large serving bowl, combine lettuce, arugula, parsley, basil, mint and marjoram. Dress with remaining 1/4 cup flavored oil and set aside. Grill salmon for 3 minutes. Place on dinner plates, mound garden salad to the side and garnish with chives.

SKEWERED SCALLOPS
WITH CANTALOUPE SALSA

Sea scallops lightly marinated and grilled are served with a tangy cantaloupe salsa. Double-skewer the scallops for an attractive presentation.

8 wooden skewers, soaked in water for 20 minutes
20 large sea scallops
$1/4$ cup extra virgin olive oil
1 tbs. chopped fresh basil
$1/2$ large cantaloupe, seeded, peeled and diced
$3/4$ cup diced red bell pepper
4 green onions, minced, white and light green parts
$1/4$ cup chopped fresh basil
2 tbs. light rum
salt to taste
1 pinch red pepper flakes, optional
4 fresh basil sprigs for garnish

Thread scallops using 2 skewers. Place in a plastic bag with oil and basil and refrigerate for 30 minutes. In a medium serving bowl, combine cantaloupe, pepper, onions, basil and rum. Mix well, cover and chill for 30 minutes.

Heat the grill for 10 minutes. When ready, remove skewers from marinade and grill for 1½ to 2 minutes, depending on size. Place on a serving plate and garnish with basil sprigs. Pass the salsa.

SCALLOPS WITH
HORSERADISH DILL SAUCE

Perky horseradish adds spice to the dill-flavored tartar sauce. Once again scallops are attractively double-skewered.

3/4 cup mayonnaise
2 tbs. commercially prepared creamy horseradish sauce
1 tbs. lime juice
3 tbs. chopped fresh dill
1/4 cup chopped sweet pickles
2 tbs. capers, rinsed and drained
olive oil spray
8 skewers, soaked in water for 20 minutes
1/4 lb. thinly sliced prosciutto
20 large sea scallops
2 tbs. extra virgin olive oil
salt and white pepper to taste

In a small serving bowl, mix mayonnaise, horseradish, lime juice, 2 tbs. of the dill, pickles and capers. Set aside.

Mist the cold grill with oil and heat for 10 minutes. Cut prosciutto into 25 pieces and thread alternately with scallops. Spread oil in a shallow dish and mix with remaining 1 tbs. dill. Dip skewers into oil mixture, coating thoroughly. When ready, cook in hot grill for 1½ to 2 minutes, depending on scallop size. Serve with horseradish sauce.

BLACK TIGER SHRIMP WITH GINGER

This easy-to-prepare dish features tangy, succulent shrimp rich with the fragrance of ginger. Serve with green beans and steamed jasmine rice.

1 1/2 lb. large tiger shrimp
1 tsp. sea salt
3 tbs. peanut oil
2 tbs. mirin rice wine
1 tbs. grated fresh ginger
2 cloves garlic, minced
1/4 tsp. red pepper flakes
4 lemon wedges

Under running water, peel and devein shrimp, but leave tail on. Dry, sprinkle with salt and set aside. In a large plastic bag, mix 2 tbs. of the oil, mirin, ginger, garlic and red pepper flakes. Add shrimp, coat well with marinade and refrigerate for 1 hour.

When ready, brush the cold grill with remaining 1 tbs. oil and heat for 10 minutes. Lift shrimp from marinade, blot with paper towels and cook for 2 minutes. Serve with lemon wedges.

SHRIMP MAUI-STYLE

Ripe pineapple, sweet Maui onion slices and green bell pepper combine with jumbo shrimp in this "taste of the islands" skewer. Tamari sauce is very similar to soy sauce, with a milder, less salty flavor.

8 skewers, soaked in water for 30 minutes
3 tbs. tamari or low-salt soy sauce
3 tbs. fresh pineapple juice
1 tbs. lime juice
1 lb. jumbo shrimp, peeled and deveined
1/4 cup peanut oil
1 small Maui or other sweet onion, cut into quarters, slices separated
1 cup fresh pineapple chunks
1 green bell pepper, cut into 8 pieces

In a large plastic bag, mix tamari or soy sauce, pineapple juice, lime juice and shrimp. Marinate at room temperature for no longer than 15 minutes.

When ready, brush the cold grill with 1 tbs. of the oil and heat for 15 minutes. Lift shrimp from marinade, blot with paper towels and alternately thread on skewers with onion, pineapple chunks and green pepper. Brush skewers with remaining 3 tbs. peanut oil and cook for 3 minutes in hot grill.

SPICY SQUID AND ARUGULA SALAD

Servings: 4

Although squid is most readily available frozen, the fresh flavor of the sea is recaptured when the squid is marinated in brine prior to grilling. For ease of preparation, choose cleaned squid, available in the fish department of some food markets.

3 cups ice water
½ cup salt
1 cup ice cubes
1½ lb. cleaned, small squid bodies and
  tentacles
¾ cup extra virgin olive oil
2 tbs. chopped garlic
1 tsp. red pepper flakes
1 tbs. lemon juice
2 large bunches arugula
1½ cups cherry tomatoes
salt and freshly ground black pepper
lemon wedges

In a deep bowl, combine ice water, salt and ice cubes to make brine. Rinse cleaned squid bodies and tentacles under running water and add to brine. Cover and refrigerate overnight. When ready to cook, remove squid from brine. Rinse thoroughly and blot dry. In a small bowl, mix together 1/2 cup of the oil, garlic and red pepper flakes.

Coat squid with oil mixture and marinate for 10 minutes while heating the grill. Wash and dry arugula. Remove stems and cut leaves in half. In a large bowl, whisk together remaining 1/4 cup oil and lemon juice. Toss arugula and tomatoes in dressing and arrange on 4 platters. Lift squid from marinade, place on hot grill and cook for 2 minutes or until slightly curled and juices begin to flow. Top each salad plate with a portion of squid. Remove drip pan from grill and pour accumulated juices over salads. Season with salt, pepper and lemon.

Variation: Microwave reserved marinade and combine with cooking juices and grilled squid to make a flavorful topping for cooked linguini. Including the cherry tomatoes is optional.

BASIL SHRIMP WITH ANGEL HAIR PASTA

Servings: 4

Succulent jumbo shrimp flavored with a basil-garlic marinade nestle into a bed of angel hair pasta. Tiny cherry tomatoes and additional basil leaves add sweetness and color.

1/2 cup extra virgin olive oil
6 cloves garlic, pressed
1 cup chopped fresh basil
sea salt and freshly ground pepper
20 jumbo shrimp, peeled and deveined
1 pkg. (8 oz.) angel hair pasta
20 cherry tomatoes, halved
2 lemon wedges

In a large bowl, mix together oil, garlic and 1/2 cup of the basil. Salt and pepper shrimp, add to bowl and marinate for 10 minutes while heating the grill. Prepare pasta according to package directions. Drain and keep warm. Lift shrimp from marinade and grill for 3 minutes. At the same time, add tomatoes to marinade and microwave on full power for 3 minutes. Toss pasta in marinade until well coated. Place on serving dishes and top each with 5 shrimp and some of the remaining basil. Serve with lemon wedges.

POULTRY DISHES

HOISIN CHICKEN THIGHS

Boneless chicken thighs grill to succulent perfection when marinated in this hoisin sauce base. Look for thick, mahogany-colored hoisin sauce where Oriental foods are sold. This dish is good hot or cold.

2 tbs. sesame oil
1/4 cup dry sherry
2 tbs. hoisin sauce
2 tbs. soy sauce
4 cloves garlic, pressed
1 tbs. chopped green onion
2 tbs. grated fresh ginger
1/4 cup chopped fresh cilantro, stems and leaves
1 1/4 lb. boneless, skinless chicken thighs, cut into 2-inch squares
olive oil spray
2 tbs. sesame seeds, toasted

In a small bowl, whisk oil, sherry, hoisin sauce and soy sauce. Pour into a large plastic bag. Add garlic, onion, ginger and 2 tbs. of the cilantro. Mix well by manipulating bag. Add chicken and mix so chicken is coated with marinade. Refrigerate for 6 hours or overnight.

When ready to cook, spray the cold grill with olive oil and heat for 15 minutes. Remove chicken from marinade and wipe with paper towels. Grill for 3 to 4 minutes. Sprinkle with sesame seeds and remaining 2 tbs. cilantro before serving.

LEMON CHICKEN WITH PASTA

Servings: 6

Plan ahead to marinate the chicken overnight for the most intense lemon flavor.

$\frac{1}{2}$ cup extra virgin olive oil
$\frac{1}{2}$ cup dry white wine
$\frac{1}{2}$ cup plus 2 tbs. minced fresh flat-leaf parsley
3 cloves garlic, minced
3 tbs. lemon juice
1 tbs. lemon zest
2 lb. boneless, skinless chicken breasts
$\frac{1}{2}$ cup chicken broth
3 tbs. unsalted butter
1 pkg. (16 oz.) linguini
1 tbs. capers, rinsed and drained
$\frac{1}{4}$ cup grated Parmesan cheese

In a large plastic bag, mix oil, wine, $\frac{1}{2}$ cup of the parsley, garlic, lemon juice and zest. Add chicken. Mix well and refrigerate overnight. Lift chicken from marinade, lightly blot with paper towels and set aside.

Pour marinade into a microwave-safe bowl. Add chicken broth and cook on full power for 5 minutes, or until reduced and slightly thickened. Strain marinade, discard solids, stir in butter, cover and keep warm.

Cook linguini according to package directions. Strain and place in a large oven-safe serving dish. Toss with reduced marinade and hold in a 200° oven. Heat the grill and cook chicken for 4 minutes. Remove to a work surface and cut into thin slices.

Fan slices out on linguini, sprinkle with capers and top with cheese and remaining 2 tbs. parsley.

MOROCCAN CHICKEN
WITH GINGER SALSA

Cinnamon is a popular ingredient in Moroccan cooking. This slightly sweet, aromatic rub combines cinnamon, nutmeg, allspice and freshly ground black pepper for zest.

2 tsp. garlic powder
2 tsp. cinnamon
1 tsp. freshly ground allspice
$1/2$ tsp. freshly grated nutmeg
1 tsp. freshly grated black pepper
$1^1/4$ lb. mixed boneless, skinless chicken breasts and thighs
Ginger Salsa, follows

In a small shallow dish, mix garlic, cinnamon, allspice, nutmeg and pepper. Cut chicken into 2-inch pieces, no more than $1/2$-inch thick. Dip chicken in spice mixture and pat it into the flesh. Set aside at room temperature while making salsa. Mist the grill with olive oil and heat for 10 minutes. Grill chicken for 3 to 4 minutes. Serve with *Ginger Salsa*.

GINGER SALSA

3 large Roma tomatoes, chopped
1 tbs. minced fresh ginger
1/4 cup minced green onions
1/4 cup minced fresh cilantro
1 tsp. lemon juice
1 pinch red pepper flakes
salt and pepper to taste

In a serving bowl, combined tomatoes, ginger, onions, cilantro, lemon juice, red pepper flakes, salt and pepper. Mix well.

CHICKEN WITH ALMOND SAUCE

This unusual sauce, inspired by the Spanish Moors, is thickened with spiced, crushed almonds and toasted breadcrumbs.

1/4 cup plus 2 tbs. extra virgin olive oil
1 1/2 tbs. minced garlic
salt and white pepper to taste
1 1/2 lb. boneless, skinless chicken pieces, cut into 1/2-inch-thick slices
1 tbs. toasted breadcrumbs
1/4 cup almonds, toasted
3 tbs. finely chopped fresh parsley
3/4 cup chicken stock
1/4 cup sherry wine
2 strands saffron, soaked in a little stock
1/4 tsp. ground allspice
1/8 tsp. ground cloves

In a shallow utility dish, mix ¼ cup of the oil, 1 tbs. of the garlic, salt and pepper. Coat chicken with oil mixture and let stand at room temperature while preparing sauce. In a blender container, combine remaining 2 tbs. oil, remaining 1 tbs. garlic, breadcrumbs, almonds and 2 tbs. of the parsley. Whirl in blender until a paste forms. Gradually add stock, wine, saffron, allspice and cloves. Whirl to blend. Pour sauce into a microwave-safe bowl. Microwave on full power for 2 minutes or until thickened. Set aside.

Heat the grill for 15 minutes. Cook chicken for 3 to 4 minutes. Remove to a serving dish and sprinkle with remaining 2 tbs. parsley. Serve sauce separately.

CHINESE GARLIC CHICKEN

Boneless, skinless chicken breasts star in this easy-to-prepare entrée. Plum sauce or duck sauce, a thick, sweet-sour condiment made with plums, apricots, sugar and seasoning, is available where Oriental foods are sold.

1 tbs. Chinese five-spice powder
1 tsp. garlic powder
1 tsp. ground coriander
4 boneless, skinless chicken breast halves
2 tbs. peanut oil
1/4 cup plum sauce

In a small cup, mix five-spice powder, garlic and coriander. Cut each half breast into 2 cutlets. Place cutlets between two slices of plastic wrap, flatten slightly with a meat mallet and rub with spice mixture. Refrigerate for 30 minutes.

Lightly coat the cold grill with peanut oil and heat for 15 minutes. Bring chicken to room temperature and grill for 2 to 3 minutes, or until cooked. Serve with plum sauce.

CHICKEN AND HAM SKEWERS

Servings: 4

Chicken, mushrooms, ham and peppers—this diverse combination of flavors and textures brings interest to a weeknight dinner. Oven fries and a green salad complete the picture.

8 wooden skewers
olive oil spray
1 lb. boneless, skinless chicken, cut into 1/2-inch-thick slices
1/2 lb. boneless ham, cut into 1/4-inch slices
1/2 lb. fresh white mushrooms
1 green bell pepper, seeded, ribs removed and cut into thin pieces
1/4 cup olive oil
2 cloves garlic, pressed
salt and freshly ground black pepper to taste

Soak wooden skewers in hot water for 30 minutes. Mist the cold grill with oil and heat for 15 minutes. When ready, thread alternating pieces of chicken, ham, mushrooms and pepper on skewers. Leave a small space between chicken pieces to ensure even cooking. In a shallow dish, mix oil, garlic, salt and pepper. Coat skewers well with mixture and grill for 4 minutes.

DIJON CHICKEN

Tarragon heightens the peppery flavor of Dijon mustard in this easy-to-prepare entrée. For a colorful presentation, garnish grilled chicken with fresh tarragon sprigs and cherry tomatoes.

1/4 cup extra virgin olive oil
1 tbs. Dijon mustard
1 tbs. lemon juice
1 tbs. chopped fresh tarragon, or 2 tsp. dried
4 boneless, skinless chicken breast halves

In a plastic bag, combine 3 tbs. of the oil, mustard, lemon juice and tarragon. Mix well by manipulating bag. Add chicken and coat with marinade. Refrigerate for 30 minutes or up to 6 hours.

When ready, bring chicken to room temperature. Lift chicken from marinade and wipe with paper towels. Spread remaining 1 tbs. oil over chicken and cook in the hot grill for 3 to 4 minutes.

TURKEY BREAST WITH CURRY

Boneless turkey cutlets take on exotic flavors with this spicy, tangy marinade.

2 tbs. canola oil
2 tsp. lime juice
3 cloves garlic, minced
1 tsp. curry powder
1 tsp. ground ginger
salt and white pepper to taste
1 1/4 lb. turkey breast, cut into four 1/2-inch-thick cutlets
1 cup commercially prepared mango chutney

In a plastic bag, mix oil, lime juice, garlic, curry powder, ginger, salt and pepper. Add turkey cutlets, coat with mixture and set aside. Heat the grill for 15 minutes. Lift cutlets from marinade and cook in hot grill for 4 minutes. Serve with chutney.

GARLICKY TURKEY BURGERS

Fennel seeds and sherry wine add a sweet nutty flavor to these burgers. Use ground turkey leg and thigh meat for the juiciest burgers.

1 lb. ground turkey, dark meat only
3 cloves garlic, pressed
1 tsp. poultry seasoning
1 tsp. crushed fennel seeds
$1/2$ cup breadcrumbs
salt and freshly ground black pepper
1 egg, slightly beaten
2 tbs. sherry wine
3 tbs. canola oil
$1/4$ cup pomegranate jelly

In a large bowl, mix all ingredients except canola oil and pomegranate jelly. Form into 4 burgers, $3/4$-inch thick. Brush with 2 tbs. of the canola oil. Brush the cold grill with remaining 1 tbs. canola oil and heat for 10 minutes. Cook burgers for 4 to 5 minutes. Serve with pomegranate jelly.

SAKE DUCK BREASTS

Servings: 4

The flavors of Japanese cuisine shine in this easily prepared entrée. Look for duck breasts in the frozen food section of most food markets. Fresh duck is available in Asian markets.

2 boneless duck breasts
2 tbs. sake
1 tbs. sesame oil
3 tbs. sherry wine
1 tbs. tamari or low-salt soy sauce
1 tbs. chopped shallots

1 tbs. chopped fresh ginger
olive oil spray
$1/4$ cup prepared sweet pickled sliced
   ginger
4 fresh cilantro sprigs for garnish

If frozen, defrost breasts. With a sharp knife, remove skin and cut each breast in half. Set aside. In a large bag, mix sake, oil, wine, tamari, shallots and ginger. Add duck breast halves and coat with marinade. Refrigerate for 6 hours.

When ready, mist the grill with olive oil and heat for 10 minutes. Lift breasts from marinade, blot with paper towels and cook in hot grill for 3 to 4 minutes. Place on a serving plate and garnish with pickled ginger and cilantro.

GRILLED DUCK BREAST
WITH MIXED BABY GREENS

Servings: 4

Our version of this classic bathes the duck in a mustard brandy-based herbal marinade. Shaved dry Monterey Jack cheese and toasted hazelnuts add interest to the greens.

3 cloves garlic, pressed
2 tbs. chopped fresh rosemary
2 tbs. brandy
1 tbs. lemon juice
1 tsp. Coleman's mustard or any hot mustard
2 duck breast halves
1/4 cup hazelnut oil
2 tbs. raspberry vinegar
salt and ground white pepper to taste
6 cups mixed baby salad greens
olive oil spray
1/4 cup shaved dry Monterey Jack cheese
2 tbs. chopped roasted hazelnuts

In a large plastic bag, mix 2 cloves of the garlic, rosemary, brandy, lemon juice, and mustard. Add duck breast halves and mix well. Marinate for 4 hours.

When ready, prepare salad. In a large bowl, combine remaining garlic with oil, vinegar, salt and pepper. Arrange greens on top, but do not mix with dressing.

Mist the cold grill with oil and heat for 10 minutes. Lift duck from marinade, blot with paper towels and mist with oil. Grill for 3 to 4 minutes. Remove to a work surface and carve into thin slices. Toss salad. Arrange on a serving platter and fan duck slices over greens. Top with cheese and nuts.

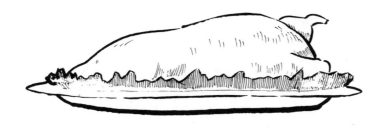

QUAIL AND POLENTA

Based on the Northern Italian classic, quail is marinated overnight, quickly grilled and served over creamy polenta with herbed cranberry sauce.

8 quail
1 1/2 cups vermouth
1/2 cup chopped fresh sage leaves, packed
1/2 cup plus 1 tbs. finely chopped fresh rosemary leaves, packed
1 tsp. freshly ground black pepper
1 can (16 oz.) whole cranberry sauce
Polenta from the Microwave, follows
3 tbs. extra virgin olive oil
fresh sage sprigs for garnish

Split quail down back, removing backbone. Cut through each breast, forming 2 halves, and flatten. Continue until all quail are prepared. Place quail halves in a large plastic bag. Add vermouth, sage, rosemary and pepper. Refrigerate overnight. In a small serving dish, mix cranberry sauce with remaining 1 tbs. rosemary. Cover and refrigerate.

Before grilling, prepare polenta and keep warm. Brush the cold grill with 1 tbs. of the oil and heat for 10 minutes. When ready, brush quail with remaining oil and grill in batches for 3 to 5 minutes, depending on size. Meat should be moist but not bloody. Serve over a bed of polenta and garnish with sage. Pass herbed cranberry sauce.

POLENTA FROM THE MICROWAVE

Makes 5 cups

4 cups water
1¼ cups polenta
2 tsp. salt
2 tbs. unsalted butter
1 tsp. freshly ground black pepper

In a microwave-safe bowl, combine water, polenta and salt. Microwave uncovered on full power for 10 to 12 minutes, stirring once. Stir in butter and pepper. Keep warm until ready to serve.

HOT BLACKENED GAME HENS

"Pollo alla diavola" (devilled or spicy chicken) is a classic Tuscan preparation. Young chickens are halved, flattened, seasoned with red pepper, weighed down with bricks and blackened on the open grill. The contact grill does an admirable job indoors without the fuss and bother of weights and brick-turning.

2 Cornish game hens
1/4 cup extra virgin olive oil
3 tsp. red pepper flakes
2 tbs. chopped fresh rosemary leaves
sea salt to taste
lemon wedges for garnish

Using a heavy knife, split hens in half, removing back bone and giblets. Place halves between two sheets of plastic wrap and flatten with a meat mallet. In a small bowl, mix 3 tbs. of the oil, red pepper flakes and rosemary. Rub mixture into both sides of hens and let stand at room temperature for 1 hour.

Place the grill under a vent or near an open window since hens may smoke during grilling. Brush remaining 1 tbs. oil on cold grill and heat for 15 minutes. Grill hens for 12 minutes or until blackened. Serve with lemon wedges.

GRILLED VEGETABLES

ASPARAGUS WITH TWO DRESSINGS

Sweet and tart dressings both complement asparagus. Select fairly large spears of asparagus for best results, and lay in the grooves of the grill for faster cooking. Serve with Tarragon Butter, *page 119, or* Lemon Yogurt Dressing, *page 119.*

olive oil spray
1 ½ lb. asparagus spears

Mist the cold grill with oil and heat for 10 minutes. When ready, arrange asparagus in grooves and grill for 4 to 5 minutes, or until tender.

TARRAGON BUTTER

Makes ¼ cup

2 tbs. unsalted butter
2 tbs. chopped fresh tarragon

Bring butter to room temperature and mix with tarragon.

LEMON YOGURT DRESSING

Makes ¼ cup

¼ cup plain nonfat yogurt
1 tsp. chopped lemon zest
1 tbs. minced fresh flat-leaf parsley
½ tsp. minced fresh chives

Mix all ingredients together in a small serving bowl.

ARTICHOKES WITH HERBS

Artichoke hearts grill crunchy-tender—that is, the heart is tender, but the short leaves remain somewhat crunchy. The lemon herb marinade infuses the artichokes with flavor and smoothness, making them good companions for grilled lamb dishes.

$1/4$ cup extra virgin olive oil
2 tbs. lemon juice
1 tbs. finely chopped lemon zest
2 tbs. finely chopped shallots
$1/4$ cup finely minced mixed fresh herbs: parsley, marjoram, tarragon and
   rosemary
2 pkgs. (4 oz. each) frozen artichoke hearts, thawed

In a medium bowl, whisk together oil, lemon juice, zest, shallots and herbs. Rinse, pat dry artichoke hearts, place in dressing and marinate for 30 minutes.

Heat the grill for 10 minutes. Place artichokes in hot grill and cook for 5 minutes. Serve warm with additional dressing if desired.

CABBAGE WITH MUSTARD

Grilling cabbage caramelizes its natural sugars. The honey mustard intensifies this sweetness, making it a popular dish with children.

olive oil spray
2 tbs. olive oil
1 clove garlic, minced
2 tsp. honey mustard
1 medium head cabbage

Mist the cold grill with olive oil spray and heat for 10 minutes. In a shallow serving dish, whisk olive oil, garlic and mustard until well mixed. Set aside. Cut cabbage in 2-inch-thick wedges, keeping a portion of the core intact. Lightly spray with oil and arrange in the heated grill. Cook for 5 minutes. Fold into mustard dressing. Serve at room temperature.

BABY BOK CHOY WITH OYSTER SAUCE

Bok choy, sometimes called Chinese white cabbage, is an oblong-shaped, mild cabbage with a crisp, mustard-like flavor. Baby bok choy, a small, tender-leafed variety with a pleasant nutty flavor, is a natural mate for grilled Asian-style entrées. Look for it in the produce section of most food markets year-round. Oyster sauce is found in the Asian foods section of large grocery stores.

12 firm, tightly packed heads baby bok choy
3 tbs. peanut oil
$\frac{1}{2}$ tsp. salt
$\frac{1}{4}$ cup commercially prepared oyster sauce

Cut bok choy in half vertically if they are thicker than $1\frac{1}{2}$ inches in diameter. In a shallow dish, whisk together oil and salt. Dip bok choy into dressing to lightly coat outer leaves. Cook in the hot grill for 2 to 3 minutes or until grill marks appear. Pour oyster sauce into a pitcher and serve with hot bok choy.

EGGPLANT WITH GARDEN HERBS

Eggplant grills to a creamy softness complemented by extra virgin olive oil and aromatic fresh herbs. This dish is excellent with other grilled foods or as an appetizer with bruschetta.

6 tbs. extra virgin olive oil
2 medium eggplants
1 tsp. red wine vinegar
$1/2$ tsp. garlic powder
$1/4$ cup chopped fresh herbs: parsley, marjoram, tarragon and mint

Brush the cold grill with 2 tbs. of the oil and heat for 10 minutes. Cut eggplant crosswise in $1/2$-inch slices and brush with 2 tbs. of the oil. Arrange in grill and cook for 3 minutes until eggplant is soft with light grill marks. Remove to a serving plate. Mix vinegar and garlic powder with remaining 2 tbs. oil. Lightly brush grilled eggplant with oil and vinegar mixture and sprinkle with herbs. Continue grilling and layering until all eggplant is cooked and dressed. Serve warm or at room temperature.

GREEK-STYLE EGGPLANT

Bring the scents and flavors of the Aegean into your kitchen with this simply-prepared dish.

olive oil spray
1/2 cup extra virgin olive oil
2 tsp. lemon juice
2 cloves garlic, pressed
1 tbs. dried oregano
1/4 tsp. red pepper flakes
2 medium eggplant
1/4 cup crumbled feta cheese
pita bread

Mist the cold grill with oil and heat for 10 minutes. In a shallow serving dish, whisk together oil, lemon juice, garlic, oregano and red pepper flakes. Set aside. Remove ends from eggplant and, leaving skin on, cut horizontally into 1/2-inch slices. Mist eggplant slices on both sides with olive oil spray. Grill for 7 to 8 minutes. Place grilled eggplant in dressing. Continue grilling until all eggplant is cooked. Lift eggplant from dressing onto individual serving platters, top with crumbled cheese and serve with pita bread.

MISO-GLAZED EGGPLANT

Servings: 4

Slices of small Japanese eggplant are brushed with lime-thinned miso paste, creating a memorable, crusty, salty-tart flavor. Miso can be found in Japanese markets and health food stores. Miso is a soy paste that can be used as a base for soups as well as a flavoring for foods. It adds richness to meats and vegetables, is easily digested and highly nutritional. Refrigerate in a covered container for long term storage.

1/4 cup light miso paste (yellow or red)
1 tbs. lime juice
3 tbs. sake rice wine
1 tbs. honey

1/4 cup peanut oil
4 Japanese eggplants
4 sprigs fresh cilantro

In a medium bowl, combine miso, lime juice, sake, honey and 2 tbs. of the oil. Stir with a wooden spoon until well mixed. Set aside. Brush the cold grill with remaining 2 tbs. oil and heat for 10 minutes. Remove top, bottom and vertical end slices from eggplants to expose flesh. Discard trimmings. Slice eggplants vertically into 3 slices about 1/2-inch thick. Brush miso mixture on both sides of eggplant slices, place in grill and cook for 5 minutes. Serve garnished with cilantro sprigs.

GRILLED NEW POTATOES

New potatoes cook well in the indoor grill without parboiling if they are sliced no thicker than 1/4 inch. There are many varieties from which to choose: white rose, fingerling, Yukon gold, yellow Finn, etc. Grilling time varies with the type of potato. Small white rose potatoes cook the fastest.

1 1/4 lb. new potatoes, cut into 1/4-inch slices
2 tbs. canola oil
1/2 tsp. sea salt
1/4 tsp. ground white pepper
2 tbs. chopped mixed fresh herbs or parsley

In a large locking plastic bag, combine potatoes, oil, salt, pepper and herbs. Seal bag and shake to coat potatoes with mixture. Lift potatoes from oil mixture, place in the grill and cook for 12 minutes until potatoes are soft with light grill marks. Serve immediately.

LAVENDER-SCENTED POTATOES

Servings: 4

Parboiling the potatoes with fresh lavender subtly flavors the potatoes and pleasingly modifies the texture. The raspberry vinaigrette adds the finishing touch to this unusual dish.

6 waxy potatoes
2 tbs. chopped fresh lavender flowers and leaves
1 tsp. salt
olive oil spray
1/4 cup extra virgin olive oil
1 tbs. raspberry vinegar
salt and white pepper to taste

In a large saucepan, combine potatoes and 1 tbs. of the lavender. Cover with water and bring to a boil. Add salt, lower heat and cook briskly until potatoes begin to soften. Cooking time depends on potato size. Do not fully cook. Drain potatoes and cool in a cold water bath. Peel and cut in half. Lightly spray with olive oil and grill for 5 minutes.

In a shallow serving dish, whisk oil, vinegar, salt, pepper and remaining 1 tbs. lavender. Fold grilled potatoes into dressing. Serve at room temperature.

SWEET POTATOES WITH GARLIC SAGE BUTTER

Partially cook sweet potatoes in the microwave or on the stovetop for successful grilling.

3 sweet potatoes
2 tbs. unsalted butter
1 tbs. minced fresh sage leaves
1 clove garlic, pressed
olive oil spray

Bring butter to room temperature. Place in a small bowl and cream with garlic. Fold in sage and set aside. Peel sweet potatoes, prick with a fork and place on paper towels in microwave oven. Cook on high power for 5 minutes or until barely tender. Remove and cool.

Spray the cold grill with olive oil and heat for 10 minutes. On a work surface, cut potatoes into $1/4$-inch slices. Spray with olive oil and grill for 5 minutes. Remove cooked potatoes to a heated serving dish and continue grilling until all potatoes are cooked. Fold sage butter over hot potatoes and serve immediately.

GRILLED SWEET ONIONS

Remember these fragrant onions when you grill steak, since they can be grilled before the steaks and served with them.

2 medium Vidalia, Maui or other sweet onions
1/4 cup extra virgin olive oil
2 tbs. balsamic vinegar
1 clove garlic, minced
1 tbs. chopped fresh rosemary leaves

In a large shallow dish, whisk together oil, vinegar, garlic and rosemary. Peel and cut onions into 1/2-inch-thick slices. Gently fold into dressing and marinate for 20 minutes. Lift onions from marinade and cook in the hot grill for 10 minutes. Serve with marinade, if desired.

RED ONIONS WITH BLUE CHEESE WALNUT VINAIGRETTE

Sweet red onions shine when topped with this creamy vinaigrette. Soak onion slices in ice water for 30 minutes to remove harshness. Dry onions before grilling.

2 red onions, peeled and cut into 1/2-inch slices
ice water and ice cubes
2 tbs. olive oil
1 tbs. walnut oil
1 tbs. commercially prepared nonfat blue cheese dressing
1 tbs. balsamic vinegar
salt and pepper to taste
2 tbs. finely chopped fresh sage leaves
olive oil spray
1/4 cup coarsely chopped toasted walnuts

Carefully arrange onion slices one layer deep in a large shallow baking dish. Cover with ice water and add a few ice cubes to keep water chilled. Soak for 30 minutes.

In a large serving bowl, whisk together oils, blue cheese dressing, vinegar, salt, pepper and 1 tbs. of the sage leaves. Set aside. Spray the cold grill with olive oil and heat for 10 minutes. Remove onion slices, taking care not to separate them into rings. Pat dry with paper towels and spray with oil. Grill for 3 to 4 minutes. Fold into vinaigrette. Top with walnuts and remaining 1 tbs. sage. Serve at room temperature.

GRILLED AVOCADO
WITH MAUI ONIONS

Servings: 4–6

This unusual combination of avocado, sweet onion and dry roasted peanuts presents a contrast of flavors and textures. Serve it alone with other grilled food or on a bed of peppery arugula.

3 tbs. olive oil
2 tbs. balsamic vinegar
1 clove garlic, pressed
1 tbs. dried tarragon
sea salt and freshly ground pepper to taste
1 large slightly ripened avocado
1 large Maui or other sweet onion
4–6 butter lettuce leaves
¼ cup chopped dry-roasted peanuts

In a large shallow bowl, whisk together oil, vinegar, garlic, tarragon, salt and pepper. Set aside. With a sharp, heavy knife, cut avocado crosswise through the pit into 1/2-inch slices. Remove and discard skin and pit. Place avocado slices in oil mixture. Peel and slice onions crosswise into 1/2-inch slices. Place in oil mixture with avocado. Marinate both for 15 minutes. Line a serving dish with lettuce leaves and set aside.

Lift avocado slices from marinade and cook in the hot grill for 10 to 12 minutes or until soft when pierced with the tip of a knife. Place on serving dish. Remove onions from marinade. Reserve marinade. Grill onions for 7 to 8 minutes, or until crisp-tender. Arrange around avocado slices. Moisten with reserved marinade and sprinkle with peanuts. Serve warm.

GINGER CARROTS

A touch of Asian seasoning introduces a new flavor to carrots. Tamari is a mellow, less sharp Japanese condiment similar to soy sauce.

2 large carrots, cut into ¼-inch-thick strips
2 tbs. peanut oil
1 tbs. tamari sauce
2 cloves garlic, pressed
1 tbs. grated fresh ginger
2 tbs. chopped fresh cilantro leaves for garnish

Blanch carrots in boiling water for about 3 minutes. Drain, rinse under cold water and dry thoroughly. In a small bowl, mix together oil, tamari, garlic and ginger. Brush mixture on both sides of carrot strips and cook in the hot grill for 4 minutes, or until tender. Place on serving dish and sprinkle with cilantro.

TOMATOES WITH HERBS

Servings: 4

Lightly grilled tomatoes with familiar Italian herbs make this preparation especially popular with children. Serve on an English muffin for a nourishing afternoon snack.

2 tbs. olive oil
2 cloves garlic, pressed
2 tbs. chopped fresh oregano
2 tbs. chopped fresh basil
salt and black pepper to taste
4 large, firm Roma tomatoes, cut in half lengthwise

In a shallow bowl, whisk together oil, garlic, oregano, basil, salt and pepper. Spoon dressing over cut side of tomatoes and cook in the hot grill for 3 minutes, or just until grill marks show. Serve warm.

STUFFED ITALIAN PEPPERS

When long, green, sweet Italian peppers are available at farmers' markets in the late summer, try this unusual presentation. Anaheim peppers have a gentle heat and make a good wintertime substitute.

6 toothpicks, soaked in water for 30 minutes
6 long, green Italian or Anaheim peppers
olive oil spray
1/4 cup olive oil
6 pitted, chopped, oil-cured black olives
4 anchovy fillets, finely chopped
1/4 cup diced mozzarella cheese
1/2 cup ricotta cheese
2 tbs. dried currants, soaked in hot water for 15 minutes and drained
1/4 cup finely chopped fresh flat-leaf parsley

Cut across tops of peppers. Carefully remove and discard stems and seeds. Set aside. Spray the cold grill with olive oil and heat for 10 minutes. In a small bowl, combine 2 tbs. of the oil, olives, anchovy, cheeses, drained currants and parsley. Mix well. With a long teaspoon, spoon filling into peppers, leaving a ½-inch space at the top. Close top of each pepper with a toothpick. Rub outside of peppers with remaining 2 tbs. oil. Cook in the hot grill for 12 minutes, or until peppers are crisp-tender.

MIXED PEPPER GRILL

Try this versatile vegetable grill as filling for a frittata or topping for a pizza or pasta. Or serve it alone as an accompaniment to grilled entrées.

1/4 cup olive oil
2 cloves garlic, minced
1/4 cup chopped fresh flat-leaf parsley
1 pinch red pepper flakes
sea salt to taste
3 large bell peppers, mixed colors, cut into wide strips

In a small bowl, whisk together oil, garlic, parsley, red pepper flakes and salt. Add pepper strips and coat with dressing. Heat the grill for 10 minutes. Lift pepper strips from dressing and reserve dressing. Cook peppers in batches. Grill each batch for 8 minutes until crisp-tender. Remove to a serving dish. Drizzle remaining dressing over peppers. Serve at room temperature.

FENNEL WITH SAGE

The slight licorice flavor of fresh fennel is accentuated by grilling. Serve with other sage-flavored grilled entrées.

¼ cup extra virgin olive oil
1 clove garlic, pressed
¼ cup chopped fresh sage leaves
salt and white pepper to taste
2 medium bulbs fennel

In a shallow serving bowl, whisk oil, garlic, sage, salt and pepper. Set aside. Cut hard green stalks from fennel bulbs and discard. Carefully remove layers of white fennel stalks. Cut in half and parboil until slightly tender. Stalks will not be uniform in thickness, so as they cook, remove cooked stalks to sage dressing. Coat with dressing, but shake off excess before grilling. Grill in batches for 4 minutes. Return to sage dressing and serve at room temperature.

ZUCCHINI WITH PESTO

The gentle flavor of grilled zucchini is receptive to a zesty breadcrumb-pesto dressing. Place under the broiler for a few minutes to firm the topping.

1/2 cup prepared basil pesto
2 tbs. white wine
1 clove garlic, minced
1 1/2 cups fresh breadcrumbs
1/4 cup plus 2 tbs. grated Parmesan cheese
4 medium zucchini
1/4 cup chopped fresh flat-leaf parsley

In a small bowl, whisk pesto, wine, garlic, breadcrumbs and 1/4 cup of the cheese. Set aside. Cut zucchini in half and remove seeds. Grill for 3 to 4 minutes in the heated grill. Remove to a foil-lined baking sheet.

Preheat broiler. Spoon pesto dressing on zucchini halves, patting down with a spoon. Sprinkle with remaining 2 tbs. cheese. Broil 4 inches from heating element for 2 minutes, or until cheese browns. Serve warm.

PORTOBELLO MUSHROOMS WITH ROASTED GARLIC AND TRUFFLE OIL

Servings: 4

The earthy flavor of portobello mushrooms is intensified by the roasted garlic and white truffle oil. Serve with garlicky mashed potatoes and a crisp spinach salad for an elegant vegetarian dinner.

1 bulb roasted garlic
3 tbs. extra virgin olive oil
2 tbs. balsamic vinegar
2 tbs. fresh rosemary leaves
4 portobello mushrooms
1 tbs. white truffle oil
4 fresh rosemary sprigs for garnish

Separate roasted cloves from garlic bulb. Squeeze garlic pulp into the workbowl of a food processor or blender. Add oil, vinegar and rosemary. Pulse several times until a puree forms. If mixture is too thick to brush on mushrooms, thin with water. Brush cap side only with garlic mixture. Cook in hot, oiled grill for 5 to 6 minutes. Drizzle cap with truffle oil and garnish with rosemary sprigs.

SUMMER VEGETABLES WITH FETA CHEESE

Servings: 6

The flavors of the Mediterranean come through in this combination vegetable grill. The recipe can easily be doubled for a buffet.

1 cup commercially prepared vinaigrette dressing
1/4 cup mixed fresh herbs
1/8 tsp. hot chili sauce
1 large eggplant
1 large zucchini

3 large red bell peppers
4 green onions
2 Roma tomatoes
1 tbs. sliced kalamata olives
1 tsp. capers, rinsed and dried
1/4 cup crumbled feta cheese

In a deep serving bowl, whisk vinaigrette, herbs and chili sauce. Set aside. Peel eggplant and cut into 1/2-inch crescent-shaped slices. Cut zucchini in 3/4-inch rounds. Core, seed and cut pepper into 1/2-inch rings. Remove tough, dark green leaves from onions. Cut tomatoes in half lengthwise. Work in batches: Grill eggplant and zucchini for 5 to 6 minutes; peppers and onions for 9 minutes; and tomatoes for 2 to 3 minutes. As vegetables cook, layer in dressing. Remove tomato skins before adding to bowl. Add olives and capers. Gently coat vegetables with dressing and top with feta cheese.

PORTOBELLO MUSHROOM SALAD

Servings: 4

Meaty portobello mushrooms star in this vegetarian main dish salad. Serve with warm crusty French bread and a mellow red wine for a quick summer meal.

8 cups mixed salad greens
3 tbs. extra virgin olive oil
2 tbs. balsamic vinegar
4 cloves garlic, minced
1 tsp. chopped fresh flat-leaf parsley
salt and pepper to taste
4 portobello mushrooms, cut into $3/4$-inch slices
1 red onion, cut into $1/4$-inch slices
2 red bell peppers, cut into $1/4$-inch rings
$1/4$ cup crumbled Gorgonzola cheese

Divide salad greens among 4 platters. In a small bowl, whisk oil, vinegar, garlic, parsley, salt and pepper. With a pastry brush, moisten both sides of sliced vegetables with dressing. Grill peppers and onions for 4 minutes. Grill mushrooms for 3 minutes. Arrange grilled vegetables on greens, drizzle dressing over each portion and top each portion with 1 tbs. cheese.

GRILLED DESSERTS

PEARS WITH CARAMEL SAUCE

Select firm pears for grilling. The nutty flavor of Bosc pears makes them a good choice.

2 firm Bosc pears
1 tsp. lemon juice
¼ cup caramel sauce
¼ cup toasted almond slices

Cut each pear into ½-inch horizontal slices. Cut slices in half vertically and remove core and seeds. Brush with lemon juice. Cook pears for 2 minutes on the grill. Soften caramel sauce in a microwave oven and drizzle over pear slices. Top wit almond slices.

PEARS WITH STILTON AND HAZELNUTS

Once again Bosc pears are featured in this not-so-sweet dessert. Serve after a mixed grill with port or sherry wine.

2 firm Bosc pears
1 tsp. lemon juice
1/4 cup chopped hazelnuts
4 oz. Stilton cheese, cut into 1/4-inch slices

Cut pears into 1/2-inch vertical slices. Cut slices in half vertically and remove core and seeds. Brush with lemon juice. Heat pears for 2 minutes in the grill. Top with hazelnuts and serve with Stilton.

APPLE SLICES WITH CINNAMON SUGAR

Crisp apples, flavored with anise and cognac, are lightly grilled and sprinkled with cinnamon sugar.

1 tbs. granulated sugar
1 tsp. cinnamon
$\frac{1}{4}$ cup apple cider
2 tbs. cognac or brandy
$\frac{1}{2}$ tsp. anise extract or anisette syrup
2 large tart apples, cored and cut crosswise into $\frac{1}{4}$-inch slices
olive oil spray

In a small cup, mix sugar and cinnamon. Set aside. In a small bowl, mix cider, cognac and anise. Place apple slices on waxed paper and brush both sides with cider mixture. Divide cider mixture among 4 dessert dishes and set aside.

Mist the grill with olive oil and heat for 5 minutes. Grill apple slices for 3 minutes until tender. Place on dessert dishes and sprinkle with cinnamon sugar.

BANANAS WITH RUM SAUCE

This crunchy, creamy dessert was inspired by the classic "Bananas Foster" banana-rum-and-ice-cream dessert from New Orleans.

olive oil spray
$^1/_4$ cup dark rum
1 tbs. walnut oil
2 bananas, cut into quarters
$^1/_4$ cup chopped walnuts
1 tbs. brown sugar
4 scoops chocolate ice cream
$^1/_4$ cup crumbled chocolate chip cookies

Mist the cold grill with olive oil and heat for 10 minutes. In a small, shallow microwave-safe dish, whisk rum and oil. Scatter walnuts on waxed paper. Dip bananas in rum mixture and coat with walnuts. Set aside. Add brown sugar to rum mixture, mix well and microwave on full power for 1 minute. Set aside. Grill bananas for 3 minutes. Place on dessert dishes with a scoop of ice cream. Spoon rum sauce over ice cream and sprinkle with cookie crumbs.

GRILLED STONE FRUIT

Servings: 4

Fresh apricots, plums and peaches combine in this mixed grill. Serve with reduced-fat sour cream or whipped topping for a satisfying, healthful dessert.

olive oil spray
2 tbs. hazelnut oil
1 tsp. raspberry vinegar
2 apricots, halved
2 plums, halved
2 small peaches, halved
2 tbs. chopped fresh tarragon

Mist the cold grill with olive oil and heat for 15 minutes. In a long, shallow dish, whisk oil and vinegar. Dip cut side of fruit in mixture and steep for 15 minutes. Cook on hot grill for 2 to 3 minutes. Remove fruit to dessert dishes and sprinkle with tarragon.

GOAT CHEESE WITH STRAWBERRY SAUCE

This elegant dessert combines creamy goat cheese with luscious, fresh strawberries pureed with Chambord liqueur. Plan ahead since the cheese must marry with the oil overnight.

8 oz. mild goat cheese
3 tbs. hazelnut oil
1 1/2 cups small fresh strawberries
3 tbs. Chambord liqueur
olive oil spray
1/2 cup finely chopped toasted hazelnuts
4 large fresh mint leaves

Cut cheese into 8 thick slices. Place in a glass dish, drizzle with oil, cover and refrigerate overnight.

When ready, select 4 strawberries for garnish. Puree remaining strawberries in a blender container. Add liqueur and pulse until blended. Divide among 4 dessert dishes and set aside.

Mist the cold grill with olive oil and heat for 5 minutes. Spread hazelnuts on waxed paper. Lift cheese from oil, coat with nuts and grill for 1 minute until warm. Place 2 slices on puree. Garnish with whole strawberries and mint leaves.

SOUR CHERRY POUND CAKE

Sour cherries packed in luscious, syrupy juices are the perfect topping for grilled pound cake slices. Vanilla ice cream melts into the cake, adding a cool silkiness and making this a dessert to remember.

8 slices pound cake, 3/4-inch thick
1 cup sour cherries with syrup
4 scoops vanilla ice cream

Toast pound cake on the hot grill for 3 minutes or until pale grill marks appear. Fan out 2 slices on each dessert plate. Place 1 scoop of the ice cream beside cake on each plate and quickly garnish with 1/4 cup of the cherries with syrup. Serve immediately.

INDEX

Serve Creative, Easy, Nutritious Meals with nitty gritty® Cookbooks

100 Dynamite Desserts
The 9 x 13 Pan Cookbook
The Barbecue Cookbook
Beer and Good Food
The Best Bagels are Made at Home
The Best Pizza is Made at Home
Bread Baking
Bread Machine Cookbook
Bread Machine Cookbook II
Bread Machine Cookbook III
Bread Machine Cookbook IV
Bread Machine Cookbook V
Bread Machine Cookbook VI
Cappuccino/Espresso
Casseroles
The Coffee Book
Convection Oven Cookery
Cooking for 1 or 2
Cooking in Clay
Cooking in Porcelain
Cooking on the Indoor Grill
Cooking with Chile Peppers
Cooking with Grains
Cooking with Your Kids

Creative Mexican Cooking
Deep Fried Indulgences
The Dehydrator Cookbook
Edible Pockets for Every Meal
Entrées From Your Bread Machine
Extra-Special Crockery Pot Recipes
Fabulous Fiber Cookery
Fondue and Hot Dips
Fresh Vegetables
From Freezer, 'Fridge and Pantry
From Your Ice Cream Maker
The Garlic Cookbook
Gourmet Gifts
Healthy Cooking on the Run
Healthy Snacks for Kids
The Juicer Book
The Juicer Book II
Lowfat American Favorites
Marinades
Muffins, Nut Breads and More
The New Blender Book
New International Fondue Cookbook
No Salt, No Sugar, No Fat
One-Dish Meals

The Pasta Machine Cookbook
Pinch of Time: Meals in Less than 30
  Minutes
Recipes for the Loaf Pan
Recipes for the Pressure Cooker
Recipes for Yogurt Cheese
Risottos, Paellas, and other Rice
  Specialties
Rotisserie Oven Cooking
The Sandwich Maker Cookbook
The Sensational Skillet: Sautés and
  Stir-Fries
Slow Cooking in Crock-Pot,® Slow
  Cooker, Oven and Multi-Cooker
The Steamer Cookbook
The Toaster Oven Cookbook
Unbeatable Chicken Recipes
The Vegetarian Slow Cooker
The Versatile Rice Cooker
Waffles
The Well Dressed Potato
Worldwide Sourdoughs from Your
  Bread Machine
Wraps and Roll-Ups

For a free catalog, call: Bristol Publishing Enterprises, Inc.
(800) 346-4889
www.bristolcookbooks.com